FRANCIS ASBURY

AS HE APPEARED AT THE TIME OF HIS ELECTION TO THE
EPISCOPACY, IN 1784

FRANCIS ASBURY

A BIOGRAPHICAL STUDY

By HORACE M. DU BOSE, D.D.
Author of the Symbol of Methodism

METHODIST FOUNDERS' SERIES

NASHVILLE, TENN.
DALLAS, TEX.; RICHMOND, VA.
PUBLISHING HOUSE OF THE M. E. CHURCH, SOUTH
SMITH & LAMAR, AGENTS
1916

PUBLISHERS' NOTE.

THE Founders' Series of biographies is to embrace, in volumes of uniform size and style of binding, studies in the lives of eminent leaders of Methodism in the earlier and middle periods of its history. The design of these volumes is to revivify in a new and fresh portraiture the personalities and labors of the founders of our Church. In issuing the present as the initial volume of this series the publishers indulge the belief that they have given a foretaste of what the scheme means not only in renewing the memory but also in reviving the testimony of those great ones in whose hands the truths of the gospel were made mighty in the salvation of men. The hope is that through the reading of these volumes many of the men of to-day may imbibe a fuller measure of the spirit and zeal of their illustrious spiritual forebears.

CONTENTS.

PROLOGUE.

Two names are immortal in Methodism, and must remain transcendent in its history. One of these appertains to the Old World, and one to the New. The names of John Wesley and Francis Asbury are suggestive of that holiness, self-devotion, and resourcefulness of leadership which have made Methodism the most effective religious force that has appeared since the apostolic days.

The study of early Methodist biography is a certain means of preserving Methodist ideals. Truth and providence embody themselves in human life, and are thus borne across the tracts of time and space, as are precious odors in the urns in which they have been confined. This study will also lead to the development of a new evangelism. The spirit of the men of the early Methodist era was such as quickly reincarnates itself when a sympathetic contact is made with their times.

It is with a view to promoting a return to these early sources of inspiration that I have undertaken to conduct a sympathetic and discriminating study of the life and work of that apostolic man, Francis Asbury.

Icelandic spar has its lines of refraction so nearly coincident with those of water that a fragment of that crystal immersed in water becomes invisible. The personal history of Francis Asbury coincides so completely with the history of early American Methodism that one sees through the story of the apostle, as

through transparent crystal, the outlines of the age
in which he wrought. The Church was the travail
of the apostle's faith and love. American Methodists
have neither used nor honored the memory of Asbury
as they should. There is inexcusable ignorance of
his great work and of his great claims upon Americans in general. There is indeed a persistent tradition
which keeps his name familiar, and which suggests
that he is entitled to an indefinite place in the category
of innumerable saints, but there is no distinct and vital
perception of the man as the chief maker of a great
religious commonwealth of which all Americans are
either members or beneficiaries. There is almost no
recognition of the man for what he was in a pre-
eminent degree—namely, one of the makers and
fathers of the temporal fabric. So abstractly devoted
to his apostolic mission, so utterly not of this world,
was he in motive and act that his own spiritual insistency impressed the temporal lords and teachers to the
point of forgetting or overlooking the service which
he rendered, over and above his apostolic office, to the
State and to secular civilization.

The personal and official influence which Asbury
exercised for nearly half a century upon the pioneer
communities of the republic gave them not only a most
distinct religious momentum, but hedged them about
with social restraints that formative constitutions and
feebly enforced statutes could not have maintained
alone. The direct annual contact of this man of commanding individuality and holy life with the groups
of squatters and pioneers in the unpoliced wildernesses, and the sentry-like round of his personally directed
army of itinerants, supplied a lack in the civil author-

ity that, left uncured, had doomed our great Middle, Western, and Southern commonwealths to distressing moral deficiencies, if not entailments of deadly moral diseases.

It is a plain word, but a true, that Francis Asbury has not had from either the religious or the secular side of the republic a just recognition of his place and service in our national history. As for a monument, history made and protected, the Methodist Church is in evidence. But the spiritual offspring and successors of the apostolic pioneer have not even been diligent to see that his name is set upon the monument which history has built for him. Here and there a humble chapel bears that august name, while lesser names of his successors monopolize great piles, and are perpetuated to posterity by institutions of augmenting resources and cumulative ministries. Why should not some dominating minster, some monumental institution representing the combined loyalty and gratitude of all Methodism, attest its memory of the patriarch?

I insist also that a more pointed inquiry may be directed against the neglect of at least certain of the States of the eighteenth century republic. Particularly the commonwealths of Maryland, Virginia, the Carolinas, Georgia, Ohio, Kentucky, and Tennessee owe this man a secular as well as a spiritual recognition. While their fabrics endure the toils, the sacrifices, the large-visioned services of this man will be a cement and a bond in their foundations. It wants now but seven years to complete a century since his quiet going from amongst men. Surely the time has come for the payment of a historic debt.

What is strangest still in all this ill-fulfilled obligation is that no master of the pen has taken it as his crowning task to fully and historically portray this initial exponent of the chiefest religious order of the New World. More than one faithful and reverent-minded man has treated it as a work of love, but each has submitted his tribute as confessedly insufficient, and as a pledge and hope of something completer, more ideal. In the present volume I have aspired to pass at least a little beyond the boundaries of other biographers of Asbury in an effort to produce not so much a detailed narrative of his wonderful, simple ministry as to construct from the details of the narrative a portrait of the wonderful, simple man. If I shall but be recognized as a pioneer in this newer and truer study, I will count the result a sufficient reward of my labors.

FRANCIS ASBURY.

CHAPTER I.

The Peasant's Son.

THE accidents of birth count for little. Francis Asbury, the real founder and first bishop of the Methodist Church in North America, was born the son of an English peasant, and passed his early years under conditions that spoke no syllable of prophecy concerning the illustrious career he was destined to complete.

The story of Asbury's childhood as told by himself is of meager and homely detail, and he even leaves us in doubt as to the exact date of his birth. This he, however, fixes as either the 20th or 21st day of August, 1745. The terseness with which he has sketched the entire chapter of his early life is exceedingly tantalizing; but as no other hand known to us has attempted to enlarge the record, we must be content to draw from the brief and unembellished autobiography.

The spot made famous as the birthplace of Asbury is described in his journal as being situated "near the foot of Hampstead Bridge in the parish of Handsworth, about four miles from Birmingham in Staffordshire." But that was Birmingham of the first half of the eighteenth century. The Birmingham destined to see the perfecting of the steam engine and the steel furnace, and to become the synonym of industrial magic, long ago inclosed within its wide-reaching suburbs the site of the peasant father's cot, so that much concerning even its identity must be left to conjecture. But of how little consequence is this! Homer is Homer, wherever his birthplace. The main significance of Asbury's life belongs to another hemisphere than that which held the once green fields and bucolic homes of Handsworth parish.

The efforts of well-meaning biographers to amend the social rank of Asbury's family are without profit, as they are without justification. Joseph Asbury, the father of Francis, was of humble antecedents, and the lineage of his mother was no prouder. Asbury himself plainly says that his parents belonged to the stock of the common people. As a means of livelihood the father followed gardening for the rich families of the parish. Moreover, his plainness of intellect comported with his rank and fortune, and suggests no explanation in heredity of the greatness of the son. He appears to have found time outside of his days of hire to cultivate the scanty acres that lay about his cottage, itself leased from some feudal landlord. The produce of these acres, with his wages, constituted his entire income. The family of which he was the head ate its bread in the sweat of one honest face.

A somewhat sinister touch has been given the paragraph devoted by most of the bishop's biographers to the elder Asbury. This appears to have come about mainly in consequence of the absence of a definite testimony from the son, whose account of his parent is summed up in a few respectful allusions. The negative record is not an impeachment, nor even a depreciation. Beyond any doubt, Joseph Asbury was a man of real, if still of simple, worth. He had excellent points, and though evidently not of an assertive spirit, enjoyed the respect of honest men and the reverence of his own household. In such faith and sturdiness as his the Commonwealth of England has been grounded since Runnymede, and these also furnished the soil in which the seeds of the Wesleyan revival took ready and lasting root.

The mother of Asbury, like the mother of the Wesleys, was devout and actively religious. Moreover, she was, for her station, a woman of exceptional intelligence, and this counted in the rearing of her son for more than enhanced rank or fortune. Her manner was serious and quiet, and her judgment, tempered by an unfailing charity, was always clear and safe. In his maturer years the son extolled her as "the tenderest of mothers," and it is certain that the affectionate encomium was merited. The early death of an only daughter had chastened her spirit and greatly accentuated her devotional habits. In his journal the Bishop has drawn a picture of his mother as he saw her in his childhood days "standing by a large window poring over a book for hours together." The touch is simple enough, but in connection with the reader's instinctive remembrance of a tiny mound white with hawthorn petals in Handsworth's ancient churchyard it takes on the sanctity and beauty of an elegy.

Asbury's strong early moral and religious bent may well be supposed to have come from his mother, though in the matter of training their son she was not without sympathy and help from her husband. Both were zealous members of the Established Church, and in their humble home they kept alight the lamp of prayer. Nor was that home a stranger to

outside influences. So alert and spiritually sympathetic was Elizabeth Asbury that she constantly attracted to her hearthstone religious teachers capable
of imparting the soundest and most helpful instruction. In time she came herself also to be a leader of
devotional meetings held amongst her female neighbors. Thus she created about the life of her only son
unusual religious conditions, the influences of which
wrapped his after years in solitudes of apostolic sanctity.

But for the knowledge which we have of this maternal devotion and care, and the simply fervent religious atmosphere pervading his early home, it would
be difficult to receive unquestioningly the account
given by the Bishop in after years of his boyish recti-
tude. The climax of this early ethical sense is expressed in the declaration that he had "neither dared
an oath nor hazarded a lie." Scarcely less exceptional is the testimony that when his early companions
were found to be vile he could not join them in their
offenses, but grieved in secret over their impurities.
The world has had its souls of childhood over which
the Epiphany of Bethlehem has prevailed. There have
been those who were sanctified from their mothers'
wombs, nor do they belong wholly to the ancient
world. The name of the peasant's son for whom was
reserved the apostleship of the New World is not un-
worthy to be mentioned with those of Isaiah and John
the Baptist. The soul that sacrificed and toiled and
grew ever whiter and stronger preaching the gospel
in the American wilderness had drawn its life from
far-off sources and through channels of unwonted
purity. It indeed belonged to a "mysterious order,"

and employed in its active testimony "the unused and unsuspected forces that slumber in religion."

Poor at best were the educational advantages provided for the peasant children of England in the eighteenth century, but they were often rendered still further impossible by reason of the brutal system of pedagogy then in vogue. This system has been mercilessly, though only too justly, caricatured by Charles Dickens in "Nicholas Nickleby," in the methods credited to "Old Squeers" of "Do-the-boys-Hall." The master of the Staffordshire school to which young Asbury was sent proved to be a veritable "Old Squeers." The piously reared lad lacked the pugnacity of a Nickleby; perhaps he lacked a certain wholesome worldly-mindedness, and so did not resist the tyrant of the ferrule. Instead, when beaten by the churlish master, he had recourse to tears and prayers in secret, but the generation of Squeers neither heard prayers nor indulged in the foible of mercy.

Largely as the result of the cruelty which was visited upon him, but possibly also because of the absence of educational ideals in his parents, pious and devoted though they were, it was decided that the future Bishop should make his way without further training in school. Piety and probity are not always wisdom; even love, the master passion of the human breast, is fallible, often even to blindness. But when God and nature fashion a great man they not only set a sign upon his outward members, but they leave a secret in his heart which he must needs manifest in spite of lagging fortune or imperfect ministries. In a time when unseen forces wrought upon him, the son of the peasant manifested his secret; but in tender years he was withdrawn from school and did not again take up seriously the pursuit of knowledge until a maturer age and a newer inspiration set him upon the difficult task of self-help. Nevertheless, at the age of seven he had learned to read, and found in the heroic books of the Bible a literature that stirred his thought, so genuinely insinuating and inspiring are those matchless epics and chronicles of the Hebrew Scriptures.

As well as can be judged from the scrappy material upon which we are building, the cutting short of Asbury's school-going occurred some time after he had entered his eleventh year. He must therefore have had three or four years of more or less continuous training, which will account for the fairly rudimentary foundation on which his later learning was built.

An education being now no longer considered, the lad must begin to earn his own bread. To that end service was accepted for him in the house of a Staffordshire gentleman of rank and means, and, as the story goes, of ungodly life and habits. Nothing more certainly argues the humble state of the Asbury family than this going of the only child, while yet of tender years, into service. Nothing short of necessity could have induced the pious gardener and his wife to consent to such an arrangement for their son. But it betrayed their homely view concerning the career to which providence had destined their offspring. Peasants they were, nor could they look beyond the horizon of their peasant lives; or if so, they dreamed not how it might be widened for them or theirs. The social estates of eighteenth-century England were separated by almost impassable barriers. The Wesleyan reformation, more than any other force, broke down these barriers, and made of the bulk of the peasantry a great middle class in English life. It also made this middle class intellectually potent.

The entrance of young Asbury into the service of the Staffordshire gentleman was in some respects another case of Joseph in the house of Potiphar. The surroundings were unfavorable to piety, but the well-taught and prayer-guided youth escaped serious contamination, though he speaks of awakened pride as a consequence of his new relations. But his term of service was destined to bring a double reward. The family in which he served was a polite one, and seems to have affected the best code of manners known to the English gentry of that day. The courtesies and habits of gentility must needs have impressed the sympathetic youth accustomed to solitude and social isolation. He could not have been an inapt observer of the manners of the great people whom he served. At least one of his biographers is led to believe that it was during this service that Asbury himself acquired that ease of manner and action that afterwards made him appear so much at home in the houses of the aristocratic people of North America. Thus are the parables of providence expounded; thus does destiny neglect no smallest element in fitting men to fulfill her high decrees. It would be a safe undertaking to show that the stay of Joseph in Potiphar's house contributed largely toward preparing him for lordship over all the land of Egypt. So was Asbury, while a servant in the house of his rich neighbor, fitted in one of the particulars necessary to the success of his apostolate in the New World.

The good sense and religious instincts of the As-

burys probably suggested an early termination of their
son's relations to an ungodly master; so after a time—
probably about a year—the arrangement ended, and
the lad was later apprenticed for a period of six and
one-half years to learn a trade. There is some doubt
as to the character of this trade, Asbury being, as it
would seem, designedly silent on that point, as upon
so many other matters relating to this period of his
life. Some say that it was the trade of a saddler, while
others have it that he learned the business of a button
or buckle maker. It was more probably the former,
though so far as I have ascertained only one of his
biographers has adopted this view.

His new relations brought him into contact with
people whose social and religious ideals were congenial. In his new master's household he dwelt as a
member of the family, and set earnestly about the
task of learning his trade. Here is the Pauline precedent. The saddle maker of Staffordshire strikes on
the beginning level of the tent maker of Tarsus. The
affinity between apostolicity and labor is ancient and
continuous. The master workman in spiritual things
is shadowed forth in the growing skill of the apprentice who honors his craft.

That Asbury would in time have made a master
saddler may well be supposed; but God had another
use for the untaught son of the peasant, and was soon
to give him a token of that choice. However, at this
time there was neither sign nor voice, and the youth
had settled down to contentment with his lot. No intellectual longing or dream of ambition visited him.
Indeed, it is likely that the moiety of learning acquired in childhood was, with the dreams of infancy,

becoming irrelevant amid the listlessness of toilful and bookless days. These are the conditions under which the brain becomes sluggish and the pain of desire is soothed into indifference. Here begins the inertia of those millions who live and die without giving a sign.

This is not the place to assess the intellectual powers of Asbury, but a reference to his healthy mentality properly comes in here. In spite of the cruel treatment received at the hands of a churlish schoolmaster, the lad showed an early though not extraordinary aptitude for letters. But the exceptional quality—the real precocity—of his taste was in his choice of reading, though we cannot know how much of this was necessity. We cannot know if any brave tales of adventure, any high-drawn romances, were brought within his reach to be turned down for those serious and solid volumes which first entranced his soul. The genius of Asbury, if genius he had beyond "the art of taking pains," was in the ethereally ethical element of his thoughts. The Galilean light shone through them. Had there been a record of these thoughts in childhood, or had his peasant surroundings afforded any chance for their expression, then indeed might a prophecy of his future goings have been read; but even the mother heart that warmed with unutterable tenderness the life of his own could not read out the secret of the days of her son. To see him come in blamelessness to maturity, and filling at last the room of his father as the servant of a gentleman or the keeper of his horse and hounds was all she knew or dared to dream for him.

His peasant lineage transmitted to the future Bishop

2

a sinewy and well-knit frame. Though in America Asbury's body early became the prey of diseases that slowly sapped his strength, he was by nature healthy and strong-fibered. No other supposition can account for the fifty-five years of incessant labors and hardships which he endured as an itinerant evangelist, forty-five of which were spent on the rough, wide floor of the American continent, in traveling over which he averaged not less than five to six thousand miles per year. The maladies from which he so sorely and constantly suffered in America had their origin in the plentiful malaria which he absorbed during the first years of his itinerant service in the lowlands of Maryland. A wiser regimen and a better medical advice would no doubt have saved him years of suffering and preserved him in strength to the end of his days. The testimony is that in his youth the measures of sunshine and English day built into his frame shone out in a ruddy comeliness, and that to see him was to mark the heritage of a body destined to a goodly use. Described in later life as "tall, thin, and gaunt," with the face and air of a soldier whose toils had wasted early strength and impaired youthful beauty, he was in younger manhood a figure that suggested athletic vigor veiled with the contemplative manner of the eremite and saint.

Thus I have considered and put as far as may be possible into consistent outline what is certainly known concerning the infancy and boyhood of one of the most noteworthy men of the later Christian ages— a man to whom was opened such a door as seldom invites to even gospel labors; a man who, measured by the extent and results of his ministry, is preëminently entitled to be named an apostle, and yet a man, it may be repeated, upon whom heaven stole unawares with its blessings and honors.

When entering upon his fourteenth year, and having settled down to the life of a saddler's apprentice, he was without other pledge than that which covered the lives of his fellow-peasants, and without monitor or impulse to recall him from the intellectual indifference into which he had been banished by the ferrule of a cruel pedagogue. But a new and sudden influence was about to set his feet in wider paths.

CHAPTER II.

A Propulsive Experience.

THE experience which turned back the captivity of Asbury's youth and caused his powers and purposes to set in the direction of action came to him near the end of his fifteenth year. For a considerable time previous to this he had been under special religious influences, and a series of spiritual emotions had held him in a state of constant inquiry and concern. These at last culminated in a perfect illumination. While he and a companion were praying in his father's barn, he was definitely converted. It was then that he was able to believe that God had pardoned his sins and justified his soul in believing. From that moment he was, as described in his own words, "happy, free from guilt and fear, had power over sin, and felt great inward joy." Immediately also he turned to reading and prayers, and soon appointed meetings for his youthful friends whom he began systematically to instruct, while giving attention to his own spiritual and intellectual needs.

His career as a Methodist began in a most orthodox way. The son of the stanchest of Church of England parents, he was converted in a fashion particularly agreeing with Wesleyan precedents. Nor was this conformity the result of chance, or even of a general providence, but was the outcome of the instructions given him by his recently found Wesleyan advisers. He was a penitent seeking an assurance in consciousness of the divine forgiveness. To this assurance, when imparted by the Holy Spirit, not only his faith but his future destiny responded.

With his conversion emerged a longing and hunger for perfect love or entire sanctification, which was also in harmony with the new doctrine which he had embraced. This desire for the perfecting of his faith continued to be a passion throughout his after life. His journal, indeed, for the space of nearly half a century is a continuous stair sloping upward toward the chambers of perfectness. But so far as one may judge from his own words, he reached no place which he was willing to call the goal. Concerning an experience which came to him soon after his conversion, and which he for a time misnamed the blessing of perfection, he writes: "Some time after I had obtained a clear witness of my acceptance with God, the Lord showed in the heat of youth, and youthful blood, the evil of my heart. For a short time I enjoyed, as I thought, the pure and perfect love of God; but this happy frame did not long continue, although at seasons I was greatly blessed."

One of the very latest entries in his journal is: "I live in God from moment to moment." And these two entries may be taken as fairly expressive of his views and experiences in this matter during his whole life. The record does not vary in important particulars from that found in Wesley's journal concerning his own experience regarding the same doctrine.

Strikingly alike indeed in all essential details were the experiences of John Wesley and the man who stands next to him in the centuries of Methodist history. The most noteworthy resemblances are found in the sharp and prolonged struggle which in each case led up to the point of submission, in the simple inward manifestations, in the clearness of the testimonies given, in the momentary eclipse following each testimony, in the early dissipation of the doubts of each, and in the abiding vision thereafter.

The chief points of contrast in the experiences of these two remarkable men are referable to the disparity of their years and the diverse conditions of their mental attainments when they entered into light. Wesley's powers had fully matured; Asbury was still in the years of adolescence. Wesley was a priest in orders in the Church of England, a graduate of Oxford, a man of wide reading and observation, and one whose ministry had already touched two worlds; Asbury was all but untutored, was ignorant of the literature and the men of the world, and had barely traveled beyond the limits of his native shire. We shall see how significant are these likenesses and how unimportant are these differences as they affect the main fact.

The faith of childhood is always genuine and often develops into distinct apprehensions. The Son of Man not only heard the cries of harlots and publicans when they prayed no more than the prayers of little children, but also forgave the sins of those who could show no more than the faith of infancy. The beginning faith of Francis Asbury was that of a child who believed through a logic of the heart more complete and convincing than that of the proudest philosophies of men. Both Wesley and Asbury had measures of faith before the epoch-making days to which they refer their conversions. Wesley was sure of this in his own case, and made a notable entry to that effect in his journal. The roots of Asbury's faith are distinctly traceable in the acts and emotions of his earliest childhood. But with him, as with his great spiritual exemplar, there was one day when the Spirit spoke and when the penitent heard for all times and all destinies—when the currents of his life, gathering new force and volume, set full toward the deeps of God and his truth.

If Asbury appears reticent and secretive concerning the material details of his early history, he has in a few unstudied words sketched clearly enough the anatomy of his spiritual emotions. Even before he was twelve years old the Spirit strove frequently and powerfully with him; and though these visitations did not immediately bring him into a knowledge of the life from above, they did work effectually in keeping him from being led captive by the evil below. While still in his fourteenth year he was blessed with impressions yet more distinct; and whereas the former had left him only disturbed emotions, these latter produced in him a desire to obey. This awakening came through the conversations of a pious layman—a new accession to the parish neighborhood—whom his mother had thoughtfully invited to their home. But though this pious man could excite spiritual desires, he could not perfectly instruct those whom he had awakened. The thirsty youth therefore turned to his parish priest, but found him for this use a broken cistern.

West Bromich was a village of Staffordshire two or three leagues distant from the Asbury home. The parish church there was under evangelical influences, and in its pulpit appeared from time to time the most noted evangelical preachers of the Established Church. To this church young Asbury betook himself, and there heard not a few great expounders of the gospel, amongst them the discriminating and faithful Venn, and Haweis, the devout chaplain of the Countess of Huntingdon. To these and to others to whom he there listened he bears the pleasing testimony that they preached the truth. The doctrines which they expounded were steadily and surely making him free.

To his reawakened intellectual sense, which expressed itself in a steady reading habit, he owed his discovery of Methodism. The medium of this discovery was the sermons of Whitefield and Cennick. It may well be believed that these discourses did little more than deepen an already active desire, for, clearly enough, it was not possible for a youth of fifteen to comprehend them unaided. Of his mother he inquired concerning the Methodists. She had not herself, as it appears, come in contact with any representative of the United Societies; but her tolerant soul led her to give a good account of that way to her son. This indorsement influenced him to set out for Wednesbury, another near-by parish, in which the Methodists had established a preaching place, and where he had the good fortune to hear the saintly Fletcher. Although the spoken discourses of this holy man impressed him deeply and indeed fixed in his mind the ideal of a completed Christian experience, he seems to have been brought by them no nearer to a finality than he had been by the printed sermons of Whitefield. But from the first his soul was fascinated by the simple and hearty service of the Methodists. From a record of his emotions made long afterwards in his journal the following is taken: "I soon found that this was not the Church, but it was better. The people were so devout, men and women kneeling down, saying, 'Amen.' Now behold! they were singing hymns, sweet sound! Why, strange to tell, the preacher had no prayer book, and yet he prayed wonderfully! What was more extraordinary, the man took his text and had no sermon book: thought I, this is wonderful indeed. It is certainly a strange way, but the best way. He talked about confidence, assurance, etc., of which all my flights and hopes fell short."

Notwithstanding his failure to experience relief, he continued to attend these ministrations, and strove with constancy and prayer to bring his case to an issue, as he saw others do, under the direct appeals of the exhorters and preachers; but that great benediction was reserved for a quiet moment in secret, and for a place apart, which the Spirit had chosen. Both the place and experience were to become historic.

Methodism owes the force which has made it historic to an experience. That experience was a personal one; but a multitude of similar experiences, with their resulting testimonies, combined and streaming through the channels of thought and action, have operated to change the moral and religious aspects of the modern world. The true significance of historic Wesleyanism is to be sought not in the theology which it has articulated—for it has written not one credal statement—nor in the vast ecclesiasticism which it has built up, but in conditions which prevail in twentieth century England and America, and in the marvelous colonial antipodes—nay, in "the whole changed temper of the modern world: the new ideals in its politics, the new spirit in its religion, the new standard in its philanthropy."

It is but further affirmative of the spirit of Wesleyanism to say that the fact that it expresses itself and reveals its creed in the history of an experience is the fact in which it most closely resembles apostolic Christianity. Early Christianity owes its wide and successful propagation to an experience which fell to Saul the Pharisee in the olive vistas before Damascus. This is more than to say that the conversion of Saul gave to Christianity its best-equipped, most zealous, and most fearless preacher. It gave to Christianity the typical miracle of the power of Jesus to suddenly and completely transform and illuminate a human life. It also gave to history—that of the then emerging days and to all time—a force, a power, penetrating, pervasive, propulsive, and procreative to the end of the ages. The Aldersgate experience of John Wesley was in the order of that of Damascus, and simply renewed to it that testimony which had been lost by a Church long enslaved by formalism. Absolutely personal and of the order of the individual consciousness were these two conversions, but they became, in their historic aftermath, world conversions—the causes and geneses of vast epochs of human spiritualization.

By force of a divine logic the conversion of every human soul sets in motion a propulsive energy throughout the circle of that soul's powers. In scriptural regeneration the whole man answers—heart, soul, intellect, and the extraneous sympathies as well. It is transition from death to life. The man who believes and confesses must move. That movement is necessarily out of self, and hence the contagion of Christianity and the historic force of apostolic testimony to conversion.

The stress of Wesleyan theology and experience is placed on conscious conversion and the witness of the Spirit, and properly so. In that experience and testimony the movement known as Methodism really began. That this experience and its accompanying witness have power to lift and even compel men out of themselves, to attain the highest and best not only in spiritual but also in intellectual things, the lives of not a few of Methodism's greatest and most typical exponents testify. After John Wesley there is no more conspicuous illustration of this propulsive power to be found than Francis Asbury, who not only entered through his conversion into an apostolic experience, but who by reason of his faith and spirit-quickened sense rose from the lowliest of social conditions and even from untutored helplessness to a most exalted sphere of action, and one matched by an intellectual attainment that expounds the steps by by which it was reached.

A biographer of Wesley has called attention to the fact that the two great Reformations—German and English—met in the conversion of the founder of Methodism. It was Peter Bohler, the Moravian, who led him into the light of justification by faith alone. But Anglicanism, the theological system to which Wesley held, had got its confession from German Protestantism. The Thirty-Nine Articles were the offspring of the Augsburg Articles of Luther and Melanchthon, and the doctrine of justification by faith alone is to be found in each. The first historic contact of the two Reformations, that which occurred in the compiling of the Edwardine Articles in Cranmer's time, produced the letter of the doctrine; the second contact, that which occurred in Wesley's conversion, produced the fire, the life of the Spirit, and also produced the perfect type of Protestantism.

In the conversion of Francis Asbury no historical relations are suggested—that is, none save a contact with the ancient pentecostal and Pauline experiences. But the Holy Ghost acted upon the soul of the Staffordshire peasant lad in the same manner and to the same end that He did upon the soul of the scholar and master of Oxford. He put no difference between them, purifying their hearts by faith, and faith alone.

It is their religion—that is, the peculiar type of it, considered as resulting from a conscious conversion at a definite time and witnessed to by the Holy Ghost —that gives meaning to the life of both Wesley and Asbury. If this is not truer of the life of Asbury, at least the differences wrought by his experience are more certainly traceable. The personality and powers of Asbury, considered apart from his faith, and that passion of love which his faith begot within him, could never have become a world force or even an important determinative in history. Faith not only stood to him in the stead of intellectual power and transcendency, but the power of an endless life streaming out of his conversion experience wrought in him, as an after result, an intellectual effectiveness otherwise impossible. "Love taught him wisdom; love gave him power."

The lesson for the Church in Asbury's life is to be found in the fact that his power of triumph is inevitably related to his conversion, a distinct and clearly marked spiritual and intellectual crisis. The value of this lesson is not because of exceptional points in Asbury's conversion, but because of the absence of these—because it was typical.

It is impossible to discover the mental processes which led up to the conversion of Saul of Tarsus; the record is silent on what would no doubt have proved a most interesting but perhaps confusing psychological story. The important fact only was set down—namely, that it was a sudden, overmastering, and never-to-be-effaced revelation of divine power. The common marks of the highest types of historic conversions are the definiteness of the Spirit's manifestation and the response thereto of the penitent consciousness. All those lives whose testimonies have got into the calendar of the regeneration have had the hidings of their power here. In his prejustification tests Wesley observed that all scriptural conversions were sudden and distinctly marked, and it was the holding of himself to this rule that brought to him that quickening without which his life had been barren of those miracles of ministry and marvels of thought which have so greatly enriched the world. The case of Asbury makes a syllogism yielding a conclusion only less significant. The logic of the Spirit is the same.

To sum up: If John Wesley had not felt his heart "strangely warmed" in that humble meeting in Aldersgate Street on May 24, 1738, the world had known no preëminent Wesley, the man of fire and zeal, the man of pentecostal experience, nor had eighteenth century England known the quickening of the Wesleyan revival, nor perhaps any equivalent of it, and so the England of to-day had been another England than it is. If the Spirit had not in a similar manner, some two and twenty years later, visited the heart of Francis Asbury, Wesley's few sheep in the American wilderness might have perished or gone astray for lack of leadership. In that case it is not difficult to think of the New World as having been left without its most distinct and potential evangelical force. It is thus that the fate and welfare of nations turn upon the things which God brings to life in the awakening of the hearts of those whom he calls to be his saints. It is thus that his saints are made to sit upon thrones in the judgment of this world. It is thus that conversions become more decisive than battles and revivals of religion more determinative of human history than political revolutions. It was thus that the name of Francis Asbury came to be illustrious ; it was thus that he of the humble beginning and the humble faith was, at last, given so large a share in settling the life of a continent and in influencing the destinies of mankind in general.

CHAPTER III.

The Wesleyan Helper.

THAT part of the life and ministry of Francis Asbury which fell to him in England furnishes a vantage for studying the character, equipment, and work of the early Methodist preacher. Certainly the whole history of the Wesleyan revival affords no better illustration of the discipleship which through the Spirit and under the leadership of a "fellow of Lincoln College" brought its wonders to pass.

The early Methodist preacher was not as the Methodist preacher of to-day, though happily the likeness in spiritual simplicity and zeal—if still too much an exception—is not wholly wanting in the modern itinerant, nor is he entirely a stranger to the early rule of life and service. With rare exceptions, the early Methodist preacher was a layman, and that without hope of graduating through a quadrennial course of study into clerical orders. His sole ecclesiastical authority was a license from Mr. Wesley to preach in the chapels which he held for the use of the people called Methodists. Generally, too, this preacher was a man of little culture, who had come out of social obscurity, and the evidence of whose call was to be found in his own testimony, zeal, and success.

The early Methodist preachers, as regarded their relations to Mr. Wesley and the work, were divided into two classes—namely, assistants and helpers. The assistants were the preachers in charge of circuits, while the helpers were those preachers, itinerant or

local, who served with and under the assistants. The
significance of the title "assistant" was in the direct
relation which the bearer of it sustained to Mr. Wesley, who regarded himself as officially present in each
of the circuits, and therefore the man actually in
charge of it was only his assistant. The assistants
were expected to meet with him in the yearly Conferences, but it was not obligatory upon the helpers to
do so.

The letters, or license, which Wesley gave to his
preachers were meant to preserve decency and order
and secure his authority over the assistants and helpers, and, through them, over the societies. No ecclesiastical significance attached to these letters. The
Methodist Societies were not Churches; their members were supposed to belong to the Church of
England, and to the priests of that Church they were
instructed to go for the sacraments. The preaching
in the chapels and the other meetings of the societies
were supposed to be appointed for hours which did not
conflict with the morning and evening services of
the Church.

With the exception of the few who were clergymen
of the Church of England, the preachers who worked
with Mr. Wesley in England were, as we have seen,
unordained, and this was also true of the preachers
in America prior to 1784. To have suggested in Asbury's time in England that the United Societies
would one day proclaim themselves an independent
Church, and that the preachers would at last accept
ordination from other hands than those of an Anglican bishop, would have created alarm among even the
Methodists themselves. By what stretch of his fancy,

then, could Asbury have foreseen himself a Methodist bishop?

It is interesting to note the steps by which Wesley was led first to countenance and then to permit lay preaching in his societies, and at last to work it into his system as one of its cardinal features. The conversion of Wesley did not at first greatly modify his obstinate High-church views; but the wisdom nourished by the experience growing out of it did, so that before the end of his life he was completely delivered from hierarchical prejudices. He began his itinerant work in 1739 in connection with his brother Charles and George Whitefield. In an incredibly short time the societies had grown beyond the ability of these three to supply their needs. The only visible means of providing the multiplying converts with spiritual bread was in committing to the revival the evangelical ministers of the Establishment. The number of these was limited, and even of that number only a few were free to go. The situation raised a question which could be answered only from an inscrutable source.

About this time a layman violated all precedents, and greatly shocked the sensibilities of both the Wesleys by delivering, on his own motion, a public exhortation immediately following one of Whitefield's fervid discourses in the open. Soon after this—that is to say, about the end of 1739—Thomas Maxfield, one of Mr. Wesley's young converts, offered himself to serve as a son in the gospel, and to go and do as Wesley should direct. This offer was accepted not without misgivings, the Churchman yielding an evangelical inch to the new and clamorous necessity.

Maxfield was given a general leave to exhort—but under no conditions to *preach!* "Soon after," to continue the story in Wesley's own words, "came another, Thomas Richards; then a third, Thomas Westall." It will be noticed that these all bore the name of "Thomas," reversing the history of that disciple who doubted. Whatever, indeed, of doubt there was at the opening of this dispensation of lay evangelism was on the part of "a man whose name was John." Wesley did doubt, and, as the final outcome proved, concerning the steps which carried him farthest toward the success of his mission.

Again the inevitable happened. Returning to London from one of his tours through the interior, Wesley learned that Thomas Maxfield had been *preaching.* The High-churchman in him was doubly scandalized, and he meditated putting an end to the possibility of a recurrence of the offense by summarily dismissing the offender. Three things, however, caused him to pause and at last reconsider his purpose: First, his mother's caution in young Maxfield's favor; second, the fruit of Maxfield's preaching— for men and women had been converted under it; and third, his own unanswerable logic—namely, that "those who are only called of God, and not of man, have more right to preach than those who are only called of man and not of God." "It is the Lord," he said at last; "let him do what seemeth good."

But if Wesley needed a further argument to complete his conviction, it was supplied in the case of John Nelson, the Yorkshire stone mason, who had "as high a spirit and as brave a heart as ever Englishman was blessed with," and whose story is one of the recorded miracles of Methodism. An early convert of Wesley's preaching in London, where he worked at his trade, he journeyed back to his native shire to tell his kinsmen and neighbors what great things had been done for him of heaven. The simple people desired him to continue the story from day to day. This he did, and multitudes flocked to his door, where he sat to talk, and, all before he or his audiences suspected it, he also was *preaching*. Alarmed at what had happened, he sent for Wesley. The great leader came without delay, sat at the stone mason's fireside, saw the throngs that crowded about his door, and heard the message which he delivered. The evidence that a new dispensation had dawned was overwhelming, and the question of lay preaching in Methodism was settled for all time. At the death of Wesley, in 1791, three hundred lay preachers were attached to his Conferences in Great Britain, serving seventy-six thousand members in society.

Asbury's conversion was his call to be an evangelist. His first answer was to assemble his youthful companions and exhort them to repentance. This was followed by the more public step of holding meetings in the homes of his father's neighbors. These meetings appear to have been begun entirely on his own initiative. There was no Methodist preaching or oversight of any kind in the parish, or perhaps in all that part of Staffordshire. But it has been this spontaneity of Methodism that has made it effective throughout its era. The flying spark has engendered a flame.

But the zeal of the youthful evangelist was soon to be put to test. Persecutions of a serious nature arose.

As early as 1743, somewhat less than two years before Asbury's birth, Wesley himself had been subjected to much persecution in Staffordshire, at Wednesbury being attacked by a mob, and narrowly escaping death. For a year or more a condition of terror obtained amongst the Methodists in that region. Periodically this persecuting spirit revived, and now, after seventeen years, it overflowed about the feet of the latest convert, a saddler's apprentice in Handsworth parish. The householders under whose roofs the youthful exhorter had been permitted to gather his rustic audiences became alarmed, and withdrew their hospitality. Not discomfited, he began exhorting in his father's house, and continued to do so for a considerable time. Meanwhile he was also meeting a class at Bromwich Heath, and attended each week a band meeting at Wednesbury, where he had formed his first connection with the Methodists. The extent of his home labors were, however, not known at either of these places, where he was treated as a catechumen or probationer. But he was even then practicing the rule which made him so great and masterful in his work in the New World: as fast as he received he gave out. What was imparted to him of grace and instruction at Bromwich Heath and Wednesbury he quickly carried to his little hearth-stone audiences in the cottage home "near the foot of Hampstead Bridge." When, therefore, he appeared as a licensed exhorter in the Methodist meeting-houses at Wednesbury and elsewhere, the surprise of the people was great, they not knowing how he had been learning and exercising in a prophets' school of his own. It must be borne in mind that all this occurred about the beginning of his seventeenth year. It is seldom that this record has been paralleled outside of the Methodist itinerancy.

When somewhere between his seventeenth and eighteenth year Asbury was licensed as a local preacher; and although still pursuing his calling as a saddler's apprentice, he began to serve as a voluntary helper on circuits in his own and adjoining shires. For the space of about five years he continued in this relation, and thus finished the term of his apprenticeship. He had now reached his majority, and was free to make his choice for life. Like the Galilean fishermen, he gave up all to follow in the footsteps of his Lord. He left the saddler's bench to become an itinerant in Mr. Wesley's Conference.

It is impossible to determine in what circuits and, indeed, under what conditions the saddler-preacher worked during the five years previous to his entrance into the traveling connection. He enumerates circuits in Derbyshire, Staffordshire, Warwickshire, and Worcestershire as having been visited by him, but nothing is said of the time spent upon either or of the details of any labors bestowed upon them. But though these were neighboring shires, to accomplish the visitations named and to preach, as he records he oftentimes did, three, four, and even five times a week, and attend to his trade was in itself an apostolic labor.

In 1768 he served his first itinerant year as helper on a circuit, or circuits, in Staffordshire and Gloucestershire. The next year, 1769, he traveled in the same capacity in Bedfordshire, Sussex, and other parts. In the latter end of 1769, this being the beginning of his third year in the traveling connection, he was appointed assistant—that is, he was put in charge of a circuit in Northamptonshire. The next year he traveled in Wiltshire, but whether as "helper" or "assistant" the record does not show. The close of this itinerant year came with the Conference which met at Bristol, in August, 1771, a memorable date in the life of Asbury, and also in the history of American Methodism. Asbury was just then completing his twenty-sixth year. For more than six months previous to the meeting of this Conference he had been visited by strong intimations that he should offer himself for service in America. With what self-abandonment he did this, and how he was accepted for that far-off field, will be told in another chapter.

No estimate can be formed of the character of Asbury's preaching during his itinerant service in England. His journal gives the texts, and often the outlines, of more than one hundred sermons preached during his ministry of forty-five years in America; but not a scrap of any one of his sermons preached in his English circuits has been preserved. That they were crude at first, but often effective, we have reason to believe. Cautiously, and with that reserve with which he has sketched the events of his early life, he mentions several cases of awakening and conversions which followed his preaching. What, however, may be safely assumed concerning this early preaching is that it was typical of the prevalent Methodist exhortation. Asbury was thoroughly Wesleyan, and no man connected with Wesley ever more completely imbibed his spirit. Not in servile imitation of the great leader, but in a careful use of his example, he worked out a regimen of habits and industry that in some

points of excellence and practicability went even beyond his model.

The foundations of Asbury's success and greatness
as a preacher were laid in England. During the ten
years of his mixed ministry there he had mastered the
whole system of Wesleyan Arminianism and had made
himself acquainted, to a greater or less extent, with
other theological schools. The great doctrines he had
explored from the view-point of the naked words of
the Evangelists and the Pauline Epistles, and his
faith was grounded in them beyond uprooting or
change. It is certain, too, that he had read and studied much sermonic literature, and, what was still better, he had heard—not occasionally, but often—many
of the very greatest of England's evangelical preachers contemporaneous with Wesley. And here abides
a secret. Those who have heard with appreciation
and understanding the words and precepts of the
great can themselves never be less than great in
their own measure.

That Asbury during his itinerant service in England was in special favor with Wesley seems certain;
but not even Wesley could have dreamed that in his
youthful helper was wrapped up the evangelization of
a continent and the religious leadership of the New
World. It was providence, wonderful providence,
that found the Staffordshire saddler and gave him
this commission.

CHAPTER IV.

Bringing Up the Balance.

THE intellectual redemption of Francis Asbury, which began simultaneously with his conversion, illustrates the tremendous possibilities of life, even when it is shut off from the ordinary means of training and culture. It also illustrates how nearly self-help becomes divine help.

The ten years which Asbury spent as a local and itinerant preacher in England were busy years, and, as we have seen, were not without evangelistic fruits; but they were given largely to the bringing up of his neglected education. A sense of his intellectual destitution was brought home to him in the hour of his regeneration, and was doubly emphasized when he heard the call to become an evangelist. He therefore went forth into life as one who limped, or whose blood lacked the warmth of completeness. He possessed the wish, but not the wing, for flight. Not only was he humbled by a sense of his literary limitations, but naturally it became a snare to him, and seriously impeded his spiritual development. To these limitations he at one time attributed his inability to continue in the blessing of perfect love. As late as 1792 this entry was made in his journal: "While I was a traveling preacher in England I was much tempted, finding myself exceedingly ignorant of everything a minister ought to know." This was humility in retrospect.

As the newly made disciple looked from his saddler's bench down the avenues opened up by his new experience, the disparagement of his literary equipment must have been great. It is the advantage of a normally acquired education that it keeps the student's intellectual development abreast of his awakening consciousness. There is no painful sense of the unattained, mayhap of the unattainable. With those in the same case as the Staffordshire saddler, the fact is different. The constant manifestation of such a life is its consciousness of lack. But this is the inspiration of self-help.

The untutored convert began a double training upon himself, and the intellectual results partook of the phenomenon of his spiritual regeneration. In the midst of his labors as an apprentice and his services as a lay helper he laid the foundations of those habits of study and inquiry which made him at last a master in those lines of knowledge and interpretation most necessary to his work as a teacher of men. In self-acquired learning there is an inevitable lack of the greater breadth, but there is compensation in the increased mastery of self and the development of patience and self-directed industry. Patience and industry were qualities possessed by Asbury in a most extraordinary degree.

After coming to America, Asbury acquired a good working knowledge of both the Greek and the Hebrew languages. An entry made in his journal in 1777 acquaints us with the fact that he was reading the Scriptures in both these tongues. That was six years after his arrival in America. A later entry indicates that he was giving an hour each day to the Old Testament in Hebrew. It is certain that he got not even an elemental start in either of these languages during his school days; but he must almost necessarily have begun the study of one or both during his days of apprenticeship in Staffordshire.

On September 4, 1771, he took ship for the voyage to America. On that day, following the example of Wesley and the other great preachers by whom he had been influenced, he began to keep a journal. The records made in this journal give us the first certain chart of his literary goings. During this voyage he read a number of books of dignified titles. His comments upon these and upon other related matters betray a mental purpose and a clearness of philosophical perception that would hardly be looked for in a man of only six and twenty years, and especially one who had enjoyed so little training, and who had from his twelfth to his twenty-first year been first a gentleman's servant and then a saddler's apprentice. But somehow the busy rustic had found time to force his mind into habits of concentration, and had thus led captive the captivity of his own life.

Wesley himself fixed a standard for those plain, "brown-bread" preachers who came to him through so strange an ordering of providence. To these he spoke plainly when he said: "Reading alone can supply depth to preaching, with meditation and daily prayer." To help to this end he set a rule for his preachers: "Fix some part of every day for private exercises. You may acquire the taste which you have not. What is tedious at first will afterwards be pleasant. Whether you like it or not, read and pray daily. It is for you life. There is no other way; else you will be a trifler all your days and a pretty superficial preacher. Do justice to your own soul; give it time and means to grow; do not starve yourself any longer."

This rule of the leader of Methodism had transformed many a dull and clodlike recruit into a lively and effective witness before its efficiency was tested by Francis Asbury; but it may well be believed that in no other case did it work such large, such surprising results. Happily, this is not man's expedient; but is, in truth, the leaven of the royal Loaf Giver, and is still working, and working well, in the men of the newer generations, many of whom, like their earlier predecessors, have been called from lowly and untutored lives.

Few of Mr. Wesley's preachers imbibed so thoroughly as did this Staffordshire helper his catholic taste in literature; and while Asbury's literary sympathy and versatility are not to be compared with Wesley's, they were nevertheless unusual in one coming from the ranks to which he belonged. A catalogue of the books mentioned in Asbury's journal as having been read by him, and often reread and carefully studied, would run considerably above one hundred titles, and these by no means describe the extent of his excursions into the world of books. Amongst the volumes mentioned are not a few classics. The titles also cover in general the subjects of poetry, history, politics, biography, philosophy, and theology. A stray volume on etiquette is mentioned as having been perused, and the State papers of more than one publicist were also carefully studied. Of course, it could but be expected that works of theology, sermonology, and devotion should predominate in this catalogue, for he was that servant who counted the wisdom and pride of this world as nothing in comparison with the knowledge of Christ; and yet such was the sanity of his faith and the sympathy of his heart that he could see truth outside of those channels of thought which seemed to him to be Christian as distinguished from those which could only be classed as secular or pagan.

Dr. Strickland, the least critical of Asbury's biographers, says that he was acquainted with the literature of Greece and Rome; but there is little proof of this. There are few references in his journal to such reading, and the matter and style of his writings betray no suggestion of the infectious grace and harmonies of those Old World masterpieces. There is, indeed, an occasional use made of classic fact and incident; but the knowledge evinced in such statements came from general rather than special reading.

To write the whole truth is to say that the limitations imposed upon Asbury by his lack of early training, and which he so much bewailed, showed through his whole life. He was forever conscious of this lack, and it must be set down to the credit of the spirit that always strove within him that this consciousness more often turned to humility than to self-assertion, the cloak generally employed by little minds to hide their nakedness.

The cry of the saddler in the years before 1771, bewailing his ignorance, was continued as an underbreath in the life of the Bishop and apostle of the New World. If he seems careful not to disclose unnecessarily the humbleness of his beginning and his early relations, he never once laid claim to being what he was not, nor ever sought to appear other than the lowly disciple of a lowly Master. The sign is here of a greatness that no absence of the finish of the schools can discount.

For his attainment in letters he paid the price of prodigious industry; and even this had been insufficient except for his plan of work and study. His habit, when not traveling, was to rise at four o'clock each morning and, after prayer and meditation, spend two hours in reading and study. After that came a season of recreation and conversation, and then the fuller toils and open duties of the day. He was awake sixteen hours out of the twenty-four, ten of which he gave to reading and study. When on his travels he carried his library either in his saddlebags or in a small chest stowed in the boot of his chaise or sulky. Like Mr. Wesley, he knew the art of reading while traveling either in his carriage or on horseback. It was a fixed rule with him to read a minimum of one hundred pages daily. Both the purpose and the endurance of Atlas must have been necessary to support through the ceaseless changes of his days a task like that.

A nineteenth century Methodist historian quotes the statement that the ex-saddler had courted the poetic muse, and that the results of his rhyming exercises eventually made a bulky manuscript, which the author once thought of printing, but which, on the frank advice of a discreet friend, he with his own hands committed to oblivion. It is not difficult to imagine the type of verse that would come from that serious and unimaginative pen. But the fact of such essays is not without significance. Sir Philip Sidney declared that so great was his reverence for poetry that he counted no time spent upon it as lost; that though the poetry itself might be poor, the spirit that prompted it and the exercise of producing it could only be worthy and helpful. But however this principle might apply, the action of the embryo Bishop in ruthlessly destroying the offspring of his muse can only be thought of as one of characteristic soberness and good judgment. The story as told is too circumstantial to be apocryphal. To repeat it may serve a useful end. It will doubtless suggest to many the existence in the soul of that serious and unworldly man of sentiments hitherto unsuspected. Did he who was forsworn to loneliness and wifeless devotion to duty still find some abstract beauty or ideal of life upon which to lavish, in whatever imperfect note or numbers, the loyalty and worship of his chaste and chivalrous heart? Or did he, like some hermit priest, weave his reverent fancies into nuptial strophes to be laid at the feet of the Bride, the Church? At least those rhythmic hours had their place in the making of the man and the soul of patience and love that crowned his life; and the chronicler has fulfilled his office in preserving the story.

"It is needless to assess Asbury's intellect," says that most discriminating historian, Fitchett, whom we have already quoted. No more is it worth the while to attempt to discover by what processes he came to that repletion of personal force and equipment with which he entered upon his work in America. His appearance upon the stage of his future activity was like the sudden showing to Israel of John the Baptist. The first sight of him was of a man made perfect for his work. But when, where, and how? The perfected force was not an evolution *per saltum,* nor the repeated miracle of brain-born Athena; but the product of beaten fiber and of cranial gray matter whose attritions were those of the upper and the nether millstone. The uttered thoughts of the man showed the striations of the unrecorded concentrations and mental efforts of the awakened youth who had responded absolutely to the call of his destiny.

His final response to that destiny was made on August 7, 1771. Being on that day within two weeks of completing his twenty-sixth year, he went up to the Conference at Bristol and offered himself as a missionary to North America. Others had offered also; but Wesley, though he but dimly perceived the wisdom of his selection, gave commission to the youngest member of the group of applicants. With a fellow-helper, Richard Wright, he went forth on a pilgrimage that was to lead him not across the seas only, but, at last, over untracked wildernesses and through distant years to the attainment of "goals unimagined."

Just one month later—that is to say, on September 4, 1771—the two missionaries embarked for their long voyage. Asbury suffered greatly from seasickness, which was, no doubt, aggravated by the poor provisions made for his comfort on the voyage. The Methodists of Bristol had provided money for the passage of the missionaries, but had neglected to provide beds; and as the vessel was a freight or merchant ship, its cabin accommodations were limited to its officers. The missionaries, therefore, were reduced to the necessity of sleeping upon the cabin floor, with no covering except a pair of blankets each, which they fortunately had in their outfits. With reading, meditation, and daily prayers, and with occasional preaching to the sailors on the groaning decks, they finished a trying and tempestuous voyage of fifty-three days. On September 12, being the eighth day after the beginning of the voyage, Asbury made this entry in his journal: "I will set down a few things that lie on my mind. Whither am I going? To the New World. What to do? To gain honor? Not if I know my own heart. To get money? No; I am going to live to God, and bring others so to do. . . . If God does not acknowledge me in America, I will soon return to England. I know my views are upright now. May they never be otherwise!"

This was the saddler's apprentice twelve years after his conversion; this was the destined apostle, who, unaided save by help divine, had brought up that which was lacking in his mental preparation to complete his fitness for the apostolate upon which he was now so soon to enter.

CHAPTER V.

A Voice in the Wilderness.

THE first springing of Methodism in America was so thoroughly a matter of providence that even the date is uncertain. It is known, however, that early in the second half of the eighteenth century—some say in 1760—Robert Strawbridge, an Irish local preacher who had emigrated to Maryland, sowed the seeds in that colony. In 1766 Philip Embury, another local preacher from Ireland, but the son of a native of the Palatinate, with the aid of Captain Webb of His Majesty's troop, planted the cause in New York. A little later Captain Webb visited Philadelphia, then the most important city on the continent, where his labors issued in the organization of a Methodist society.

From the first the soil of the New World proved friendly to the Wesleyan doctrines, and such was their spread that laborers from the mother country were soon in demand to reënforce the volunteer evangelists. The English Wesleyan Conference, which met at Leeds in 1769, appointed Richard Boardman and Joseph Pilmoor to the work in America, Boardman being named assistant in charge. The mighty circuit, which now comprises nearly three hundred Annual Conferences and approximately eight millions of Methodist communicants, probably had then not above three hundred members in society.

Two years later—that is, on October 27, 1771—Francis Asbury debarked at Philadelphia from his long

4   (49)

trans-Atlantic voyage. With the arrival of Asbury the history of American Methodism really begins. At a glance the new helper saw that the policy being pursued by Boardman would never evangelize the country. Boardman was deficient in resources and leadership, and had no power of initiative. His spirit was missionary, but he had little talent for evangelistic movement. The handful of preachers under him were largely cooped up in the cities of New York and Philadelphia. Asbury burned with itinerant zeal. His ideal was a thoroughly disciplined body of gospel rangers going far and wide, preaching as they went. He would bring about the conquest of the continent through the foolishness of preaching. The future miracle of America's evangelization was pent within his peasant soul, and struggled to manifest itself while yet he stood at the threshold of his new destiny. To his ideal and to his tireless labors to realize it the Church owes the itinerancy. He was the first of the preachers in America to form and regularly travel a circuit.

Within two weeks of his arrival on the continent he had preached a number of times in Philadelphia, and had traveled the entire distance to New York on horseback, preaching as he went in Pennsylvania, the Jerseys, and on Staten Island. Thus he set at once the pace which he kept for nearly half a century as an American itinerant.

General Assistant Boardman appointed the newcomer to labor as his associate for three months in New York City. It was just sixteen days after his arrival in America that he preached for the first time in the pulpit of Embury's Chapel. Besides Boardman he found Captain Webb in the city, and almost immediately expressed his disapproval of the waste of labor. Three preachers shut up for a whole winter to the charge of a single congregation! He would not consent to see it. In his journal he poured out his soul in these words: "I have not yet the thing which I seek— a circulation of the preachers. . . . I am fixed to the Methodist plan."

"Circulation" was his watchword. And he proceeded to circulate. Asking permission of no one, he struck out, midweeks, through the winter snows to build on new foundations. Westchester, "a back settlement" town twenty miles from New York, was first visited. There and at West Farms he preached three times. This was his beginning. Before the close of the year, it being then near the middle of December, he had revisited Westchester and West Farms, had held evangelistic meetings at New Rochelle, Rye, Eastchester, DeVeau's, and Mamaroneck, and had also gone again over his earlier plantings on Staten Island. During January he enlarged this circuit and cultivated it with tireless zeal. But this devotion was not without cost. Exposure to the rigorous winter brought on a variety of ailments, the first of those bodily afflictions from which he suffered during his long service in America. A little constrained rest brought him relief, and by the end of February he was able to set off for a preaching tour through New Jersey. This journey, filled with evangelistic incidents, ended at Philadelphia early in April, when the first quarterly meeting for the year was held.

Asbury's example had perceptibly stirred the brethren, and especially Boardman. Large plans were laid for the next year. Each preacher was given a prospective circuit and instructed to cultivate all the land possible. Wright was to go to New York, Pilmoor was to move on the South (Maryland and Delaware), Asbury was to have Philadelphia as a cure, and Boardman was to take New England. Boardman did go as far north as Providence, and there is a tradition that he also visited Boston; but he was hardly the man to leave ineffaceable footprints in so naturally unresponsive a land. That honor was reserved for a native son of Methodism.

The entire preaching force of Methodism in America at this time consisted of nine men—namely, Richard Boardman (General Assistant), Joseph Pilmoor, Francis Asbury, Richard Wright, Philip Embury, Robert Strawbridge, Captain Webb, Robert Williams (who had come over by consent of Mr. Wesley in 1769), and John King, a local preacher licensed in America. As Asbury contemplated the plan for securing an early circulation of the preachers from the centers to the peripheries, he took courage and went about his task.

St. George's Church, the Methodist meetinghouse in Philadelphia, had been bought from a Dutch congregation unable to maintain it. It was a pretentious structure for that time. This led to its being called "the Methodist Cathedral." The property was encumbered with a considerable debt, which Asbury undertook to raise. There were a number of preaching places attached to the charge, and to these the busy itinerant added enough to make his preaching engagements at least one each day. Often he preached three times during the hours between 5 A.M. and 9 P.M. On a special tour he rode as far southward as Wilmington, Delaware, and Bohemia Manor, in the province of Maryland, preaching as he went, preaching as he returned. In barns, in taverns, in courthouses, in prisons, at public executions, and in the open he proclaimed a present salvation. Nor was his way always smooth. Not only all but impassable roads, but indifferent and persecuting hearts of men, impeded his progress. Yet of Bereans he found not a few, and had cheer without as within. Returning homeward, his soliloquy was: "I humbly hope that about seven preachers of us will spread seven or eight hundred miles, and preach in as many places as we are able to attend." Modest as that hope now appears, it was then the expression of a confidence nothing short of heroism.

Asbury was a Wesleyan—a rigid disciplinarian—and gave offense to the Philadelphians in his requirement of obedience to the rules of society. There were loud objections against his administration; but he met criticism calmly, read an epistle from Mr. Wesley approving his course, entered his own reflections in his journal, and persevered as he had begun.

It was, no doubt, well for those heroic men and their causes that they were not permitted to continue in one stay. After an incumbency of one quarter, Asbury was called away from his troubles in Philadelphia to new ones in New York City. Thither he carried his methods of discipline used in his former charge, reënforcing them, as before, with the letter of Mr. Wesley. His predecessor's policy had produced much confusion. Neglect of class meeting restrictions had been encouraged, even worldliness had not, as he judged, been properly rebuked, and these tendencies he set himself to correct. Steadily, firmly he moved toward the standard which he had set. Sharp contests arose between him and his officials; but he kept his serenity, as also his purpose, and, as was his wont, committed himself only to his journal.

These vexatious concerns kept him much employed in the city; still he found time to swing out over his former "back country" field, including the region of New Rochelle and the Staten Island district. In the midst of these varying experiences he was cheered by news of a great spiritual and temporal prosperity being enjoyed by the society in Philadelphia. So early, indeed, had his zeal for order and discipline been justified. The faithful word of correction rejected at first had at last been heeded and had yielded the peaceable fruits of righteousness.

He was just turning his twenty-seventh year, and was also nearing the end of his quarter in New York, when an important letter came from Mr. Wesley. The inevitable had happened. That letter announced to Asbury his appointment to be General Assistant of the work in America. Mr. Wesley in sending Asbury out had, no doubt, designed his advancement to this responsibility. If he had not, a single year had shown him the advantage of the appointment. Boardman lacked the qualities which his younger colaborer possessed in so remarkable a degree.

Near the end of October, 1772, Asbury started northward by stage to meet Mr. Boardman. Their conference was held at Princeton, the seat of the historic Presbyterian college. The precincts of colleges and universities were sacred ground to Asbury, peasant-bred and diplomaless though he was. If he was possessed of a single worldly ambition, it was that of being the founder of a real college for his people, and possibly the failure to realize this purpose was the chief disappointment of his life. It was natural, therefore, that he should improve his stay in Princeton by visiting the college and its pious ex-President, the venerable Mr. Davies.

Boardman accepted the promotion of his youthful colleague in a spirit of loyalty. He had, no doubt, anticipated it; but there was certainly at this time not enough worldly distinction in the position to make the attainment of it a matter of ambition or the loss of it an occasion for rancor. Whatever his feeling, Boardman certainly behaved well, and reflected credit upon himself and his calling. After a brief consultation, the preachers were stationed, Asbury designating himself to labor for six months in Maryland.

To no man so much as to Francis Asbury is Maryland indebted for early gospel seed sowing. To Maryland he gave the best labors of his life and an extraordinary measure of patriotic affection. His best beloved and forever loyal friends were those generous Maryland gentlefolk who had welcomed to their boards the blameless and unworldly youth whose only passion was the love of souls. During all those homeless years in which he journeyed up and down the continent he counted Maryland his home, and it was according to his wish that his dust found sepulture at last in the soil he loved.

Every condition at this time made Maryland the most inviting field for Methodism in all America. Its people were agreed on no hard and fast creed like that which made New England an impervious solidarity. Roman Catholicism and the English Church largely divided the population. Bodies of Huguenots and communities of dissenters also mingled in the general mass. But Anglicanism dominated, and Anglicanism was the native soil of Methodism. Yet even the Established Church was poorly supplied with priests. There were parish lines, but few churches. Probably not more than a dozen parsons could have been counted in the entire colony, and of these not above two or three had more than a show of piety. The people were either rich or well to do. Many large estates, with palatial manors and country homes, dotted the fertile districts. Tobacco, then perhaps the most profitable commodity known to commerce, was the chief product. Slaveholding had created, or perhaps had attracted from the other colonies and the mother country, a wealthy aristocracy. Abundant wealth was matched with refinement, polite manners, and excessive worldliness, not to say wickedness. The sins imported from England had mingled vanity with indigenous recklessness. Yet except in certain centers there was present little of that deadly deism which had withered the religious life of England and France during the first half of the century. But if there was no great prejudice against religion, there was no exhibition of zeal in its favor. The land waited for the coming of the reformers.

Toward this missionary Phthia Asbury turned his face. In company with Robert Strawbridge, who had already laid out a principality in the southern reaches of the colony, he left Philadelphia about the end of October, with Bohemia Manor as an objective. This had been a favorite stopping place of Whitefield's. It was a seat of colonial chivalry and the key to Maryland. Here was the habitat of the Bayards, the Bouchelles, and the Herseys, great names in the history of the colony, and not unknown to the citizenship of the later sovereignty.

The journey southward was a continuous gospel call. Daily—at the gates of prisons, at the doors of comfortable homes, in schoolhouses, in family circles, by the river and bay sides, to friends, to strangers, to masters, to slaves—the tireless itinerant opened the Word of life. Two entries made in his journal at this time will give an idea of his audiences:

"November 1.—After preaching at H's in the morning, I intended preaching in the schoolhouse in the evening; but it would not contain half the people, so I stood at the door and the people without."

"November 4.—This evening I had a very solemn family meeting, and spoke separately and privately to every one, both black and white."

From Bohemia Manor he pressed on through Northern and Western Maryland, preaching and exhorting daily, and praying in the homes which he entered. The fruits were large, though a measure of real persecution was experienced. The following journal notes will illustrate the variable fortunes of the itinerary:

"November 5.—Unexpectedly found the people at two o'clock waiting to hear the Word. I preached with liberty, and the power of God was felt in the hearts of many, though some of them were principal men."

"November 19.—A poor, unhappy man abused me

much on the road; he cursed, swore, and threw stones at me. But I found it my duty to talk to him and show him his danger."

"December 3.—Preached at James Pressbury's to many people who could feel the Word, and with much power in my own soul. Then rode three miles into the Neck, and had a solemn and heart-affecting time while preaching from Rev. ii. 11."

"December 6.—Went about five miles to preach in our first preaching house. The house had no windows or doors, the weather was cold, so that my heart pitied the people when I saw them so exposed. Putting a handkerchief over my head, I preached, and after an hour's intermission, the people waiting all the time in the cold, I preached again."

In Kent County Asbury was met by one Æneas Ross, a priest of the Established Church, who forbade him to preach anywhere within the limits of his parish. Asbury's answer was mild; but he denied the legality of such an interdict. The rejoinder of the priest was imperious, not to say insulting, whereupon the lay representative of the Reverend John Wesley informed the Churchman that he had come into those parts to preach, and preach he would without regard to the inhibition. Thereupon the parson pushed a controversy upon the visitor, and got the worst of it, which greatly delighted the people of the parish, who cared little for the parson's ministry, and paid their tobacco tithe only because it was levied by law. Asbury preached on the spot, not once, but twice, and many great people of the county heard the tidings gladly.

After six weeks the itinerant had completed the round of his extended circuit, and was back, having traveled not less than three hundred miles, and having preached probably no fewer than one hundred sermons and delivered as many exhortations.

On December 23, 1772, was held in the Maryland Circuit the first quarterly meeting in America of which we have a definite account. It was certainly the first worthy the name, those quarterly gatherings called by Boardman during the previous year being merely informal interviews at which he announced the assignment of his helpers. This meeting was disciplinary and fiscal, and permanent notes of its proceedings were kept. The characters of the preachers and exhorters were examined, the quarterage was divided, and Asbury strictly interpreted the rules for the conduct of the work. It was at this meeting that he formally disapproved of Strawbridge's course in assuming to administer the sacraments. He undertook to put the Irishman under the rule; but Strawbridge would not yield the point, and Asbury was constrained to tolerate the innovation. This was the germ of the historic "sacramental controversy," which came so near disrupting the American societies some years later.

Five helpers were present at this meeting. The colony of Maryland outside of Baltimore and contiguous points was divided amongst the helpers, Asbury reserving to himself the city and its neighborhood. Baltimore was at this time an important continental port, with probably six thousand population. The General Assistant was even then able to divine something of its future importance to Methodism.

On Christmas day, 1772, Asbury made his first entry into Baltimore. That was exactly fourteen years before his consecration to the episcopacy. From that day to the end of his life his name was closely associated with the religious life of the city.

There had been Methodist preaching in Baltimore before Asbury's time. John King had preached there in 1770, and in 1772 both Pilmoor and Boardman visited it in their rounds. It is claimed on good authority that the first society was organized in Baltimore in June, 1772. Asbury preached there for the first time January 3, 1773, to a large congregation, and with decided effect. The society was revived and strengthened, and in due time the foundations of the first chapel were laid.

As might be expected, Baltimore City served Asbury only as a base of operation. From January until the end of March he was putting in every day not necessary to be spent in Baltimore in evangelizing through a wide reach of adjacent country. Not a few families whose names have become historic in Methodism were at this time gathered into the societies in Maryland over which he had immediate charge. By the end of the year the members in society in the colony numbered five hundred, being one-half of all the Methodists on the American continent.

The winter was an exceptionally rigorous one, and Asbury's bodily ailments were aggravated by his constant exposure in travel. Also disturbing news came from the North—from New York and Philadelphia. Trouble was at hand. Human jealousies were at work amongst the saints. The youthful overseer had provoked the opposition of his older subordinates. Mr. Pilmoor was in an unbrotherly mood. Perhaps Mr. Boardman was secretly and humanly jealous. Perhaps Asbury had been unduly rigid in administration; he was reticent and secretive by nature, and had not taken the brethren into his confidence. Necessity dictated a course, and he had followed it. The future *"episcopos"* was being shadowed forth.

Mr. Wesley had been written to; both sides had written. This correspondence had created a condition which must be met. Besides, a lust for numbers had tempted the brethren in the Northern stations to again relax the disciplinary class rules. Asbury determined to correct the trouble in person, and prepared to ride northward on an official visitation. A journal entry made at this time is significant:

"March 8.—Rose this morning with a determination to fight or die; and spent an hour in earnest prayer. Lord, keep me ever watchful."

A second quarterly meeting for the Maryland Circuit was called and held at Susquehanna March 29. The work was found to be prosperous, and everything was set in order. Strict obedience to discipline was again demanded. Strawbridge had already agreed to desist from administering the sacraments, and a good understanding obtained. The helpers were again assigned, and Asbury proceeded, after a brief time, on his visitation to the disturbed societies in New York and Philadelphia. From the middle of April to the first of June he spent his time between these two cities, enforcing discipline or earnestly endeavoring to do so, according to the Wesleyan standard, and evangelizing in the intermediate regions.

Naturally this was to him a time of great stress and concern; but his journal breathes a spirit of confidence and serene courage; and it is doubtful if at any period of his ministry he was more active or preached with more evangelical force and effectiveness. Perhaps in this there was a conservation of grace, a providential filling up of his powers of soul and mind, for immediately before him was the season of his life's supremest test.

CHAPTER VI.

Under the Stress of Discipline.

THE American societies needed the superintendency of an experienced disciplinarian and organizer. This Wesley read from the somewhat conflicting correspondence which came to him from the field. The oral representations of Captain Webb, who had gone to England to plead for more missionaries, also helped him to this conclusion. It was agreed that a leader, or leaders, should be supplied. Webb asked for Christopher Hopper and Joseph Benson, great lights of the Wesleyan Conference; but Wesley could spare neither. After some delay, Thomas Rankin, a skilled administrator, a man of mature years, one of Wesley's trusted lieutenants, and who had also seen military service with the king's armies, was sent over to take charge of the work in America. Asbury had thus, in his turn, an opportunity to show with what grace he could accept a successor. He met Mr. Rankin in Philadelphia on June 3, 1773, and received him with great cordiality. Beyond a doubt, it was a relief to be eased of a burden which had sorely weighed him down.

Asbury was not greatly impressed with Rankin's preaching, of which he had an early sample; but he found no occasion to doubt that as a disciplinarian he would "fill his place." Of how he filled his place, Asbury's journal during the next few years tells an interesting, if still a very humanlike, story.

The new General Assistant took up the work with spirit and vigor. Almost his first official act was to call a conference of the preachers. The sitting began in St. George's Church, Philadelphia, on July 14, 1773, and was continued for two days. Ten preachers were present, two of them being George Shadford and Joseph Yearbry, who had come over with Rankin under appointment from Mr. Wesley. One thousand one hundred and sixty members were reported in society, being an increase of nearly four hundred per cent in a little more than two years. A tremendous testimony that to the labors and example of Asbury!

This was the first American Conference. Previous to this the preachers had met only in quarterly meetings; but now began that series of yearly gatherings of the itinerants that have created so unique and important a literature, and exercised so vast an influence in promoting the growth of Methodism.

The disciplinary strictness of Rankin's presidency at this Conference gave Asbury much satisfaction; and naturally, for it emphasized his own rulings and contentions during the two previous years. The categorical record recites that "the old Methodist doctrine and discipline shall be enforced." A decree also went out against those "who manifested a desire to abide in the cities and live like gentlemen." That this was meant to have pointed reference to Boardman and Pilmoor, there is abundant evidence; nor did either Rankin or Asbury have any desire to conceal the fact. The administration of that year was free from disingenuity.

Asbury had triumphed in his successor. He was full of serenity and confidence, and to add to his composed state of mind, he had probably, as the retiring superintendent of the work, been permitted to name his own field of labor. He chose Baltimore, where he had left so many great plans unrealized, and from which he had been absent but three months. For helpers in Maryland, he had Robert Strawbridge, Abraham Whitworth, and Joseph Yearbry. He was now to see the fulfillment of his hope, expressed in 1772—namely, "about seven preachers spread seven or eight hundred miles," and preaching in as many places as they were able to attend.

Within the first two hours following the adjournment of the Conference Asbury was in the saddle and on his way toward Bohemia Manor. That night he preached at Chester, and daily thereafter in places to the southward. On July 18, two days after the close of the Conference, he made this entry in his journal: "My soul has enjoyed great peace this week, in which I have ridden near one hundred miles since my departure from Philadelphia, and have preached often, and sometimes great solemnity has rested on the congregations."

The first quarterly meeting in Maryland was held a fortnight after Asbury's arrival. It was marked by no important event, except Strawbridge's recalcitrancy in the matter of the sacraments. He would not recognize the authority of the Conference to either estop or regulate him. A free-souled Irishman, before his conversion he had been a Calvinistic dissenter in sympathy, and he did not share the High-church prejudices of his English brethren. The arguments so strong with them weighed nothing with him. Asbury could, therefore, do no more than his predecessors had done —leave the honest independent alone. Asbury did not know it then; perhaps he did not recognize it after-

5

wards—for he regarded Strawbridge as "a weak and irregular instrument"—but it was the courage and independent honesty of men like Strawbridge, united to his own love of order and discipline, that gave so distinctly an American and democratic spirit to the Conference of 1784—the one that gave to the New World its most characteristic ecclesiasticism.

Immediately after the quarterly meeting Asbury repaired to Baltimore, where he began a campaign which soon made that city the center not only of the Methodism of Maryland, but of the Methodism of the Continent. New York and Philadelphia had at this time each but a single house for Methodist worship. Baltimore had already in the previous year laid the foundations of the famous old Strawberry Alley Chapel, and during this year completed the far more famous house in Lovely Lane, in which the Christmas Conference was later held, and in which Asbury was elected and consecrated to the episcopacy.

The circuit which Asbury and his helpers traveled in 1773 contained fully thirty preaching places. Besides these, the Assistant added to his own itinerary innumerable stops and detours, each of which ended in a prayer, an exhortation, or a sermon. The journal record of his goings is a ceaseless, tireless cry from day to day, from dawn to night, save for those days, weeks, and often fortnights, in which the ague and burning fevers, caused by malarial poisoning, prostrated him and made going impossible. Fully one-third of the time from midsummer, 1773, to January, 1774, he was confined to his bed in some plantation house, or in some tavern by the way, and during the first half of the next year he suffered scarcely less.

Surely, never was martyr more indifferent to life! With fevers not wholly abated, weak, faint, and with flesh and muscle flaccid from impoverished blood and depleted tissue, he would mount his horse and ride through drenching rains and miasmatic fogs, or whatever other vicissitudes the seasons brought. He was a voice, and in weakness or in strength, in pain or in joy, the cry was the same.

He hungered for perfection; but was beset by conscious frailties, and embarrassed by limitations which he labored to remove. Often he thought himself near the goal of completeness, but, admonished by an introspection, he drew back to fight another stage. This recurring record would, if that document possessed no other value, render his journal priceless as a test both of the doctrine and the experience of Christian perfection.

Methodism in and about Baltimore advanced rapidly during this year. There was a continuous revival, though the modern protracted meeting was unknown. Six services were held, on an average, each week in and about the city. The quarterly meetings were seasons of exceptional interest and power. Asbury attended these in person, and to at least one of them Rankin lent the additional interest of his presidency.

Probably a thousand people were this year converted under the preaching of Asbury and his helpers. The members in society in Maryland increased from five hundred to nearly eleven hundred. At the next Conference the widely scattered plantations and villages showed a sufficient Methodist population to warrant the organization of three separate circuits in the colony.

The personal ministry of Asbury, who had learned his manners in service and who had received his baptism and call in a cotter's barn, made fresh inroads upon the polite and godless people whose estates were embraced within his vast circuit. Mr. Harry Dorsey Gough, Captain Charles Ridgeley, and Mr. Carroll, wealthy planters and influential men in the colony, were amongst his hearers. Captain Ridgeley became an early convert, and Mr. Gough and his wife, though slow to yield, were sometime afterwards blessed with pentecostal experiences, and became the leaders and inspirational types of Methodism throughout Maryland. "Perry Hall," the seat of the Goughs, was one of the most spacious mansions in America. It was situated about a dozen miles from Baltimore, and became not only a home for Asbury and the other preachers, but was for years a noted Methodist meeting place, its splendid drawing-rooms being thrown open for that use. Later a chapel was built upon the estate, and enjoyed the distinction of being the first Methodist chapel in the New World that could boast a bell.

Philip William Otterbein, of the German Reformed ministry, comes frequently into view in the early history of American Methodism. He was highly endowed, a man of learning and exceptional spirituality. His contact with the Methodists strengthened his naturally evangelical convictions, and in his work he constantly employed their methods. Asbury came into contact with him during this year, and the attraction was mutual. Through Asbury's influence Otterbein was settled with a congregation of the Reformed Church in Baltimore, and coöperation between the two began from that hour. The result of Otterbein's ministry in Maryland was the Church of the United Brethren, an organization which is usually classed with the Methodists, and which is so truly Methodistic in spirit and doctrine that the classification is only logical.

The Conference of 1774, the second to be held in America, met, as had the first, in St. George's Church, Philadelphia. Seventeen preachers were present, and it was found that the numbers in society had grown to two thousand and seventy-three, an increase of nearly one hundred per cent over the previous year. As has already been shown, more than one-half of these were reported from Asbury's circuit in Maryland.

Rankin and Asbury were seldom able to see eye to eye. From the first the younger man indorsed in qualified terms the fitness of his superior. His administrative qualities he took on faith; but a year of observation reduced that faith to the point of evanishment. The journal of the complainant had, however, been silent—significantly so on that point. Asbury was religiously honest, and, like the good soldier he was, tried to think well of his General. In a way he succeeded, and his circumstances aided him to a degree in maintaining at least a negative attitude. He was on the circuit he preferred, amongst tender-hearted and sympathetic friends; he was in a state of constant invalidism, and came only occasionally into relations with the military General Assistant.

The Conference, however, brought them together and into conflict. Asbury spoke his mind, and Rankin administered affairs with a strong hand, and kept his own counsel. In one thing these two did undoubtedly agree. The dilettante and time-serving Wright—as they judged him to be—was to be sent back to England. Wright had been Asbury's fellow-missionary in 1771, and there is no evidence that any personal issues existed between them; but Asbury, who judged and chastened himself, was frank and even-handed with others. So Richard Wright was demitted to England under censure, implied if not expressed; but there is little doubt that both Asbury and Rankin judged him overhardly.

Asbury knew the American field and preachers as no other man knew them; Rankin knew them scarcely at all. Asbury, in addition to being naturally a far more resourceful leader than the General Assistant, knew how the preachers should be stationed; Rankin reasoned how it should be done. The widest difference of those two minds was as to where Asbury himself should be appointed. The last place which Asbury would have chosen was the one to which Rankin appointed him. That place was New York. There was a moment of revolt, and Asbury contemplated an immediate return to England; but the soldier in him quickly triumphed, and he acquiesced and joined in the general harmony. The breach between him and Rankin, however, became permanent from this moment.

Besides holding in view Asbury's belief that he was contending with Rankin for a policy essential to Methodism, it must be remembered that at this time he was little better than a physical wreck—fever-wasted, nervous, and temperamentally distressed by an effort to keep up in prolonged sickness a regimen of labors obviously too much for one in health. About this time he wrote:

"July 14.—I have now been sick near ten months,

and many days closely confined; yet I have preached about three hundred times, and rode near two thousand miles in that time, though very frequently in a high fever. Here is no ease, worldly profit, or honor. What, then, but the desire of pleasing God and saving souls could stimulate to such laborious and painful duties?"

Still later this more illuminating entry appears in his journal:

"September 18.—Losing some of my ideas in preaching, I was ashamed of myself, and pained to see the people waiting to hear what the blunderer had to say. May these things humble me, and show me where my strength lieth!"

"Asbury was half peasant and half seraph," says Fitchett, an estimate which is not discounted in the reverent view that modern American Methodists have taken of their great forerunner; but the peasant in him was only human—however far off the affinity of the seraphic—and the revelation of that human likeness makes his example all the more valuable to his spiritual offspring.

New York, though one of the two earliest fields of Methodism in the New World, had proven to be one of the least fruitful. It had been Asbury's first American charge, and there he had had his most harassing experiences. There he had contended for discipline and "old Methodism," and had withstood, and been withstood by, worldly-minded saints. He was, however, on his return to a second incumbency, received with love and many tokens of appreciation, though he was made to realize that the roots of the old resentment had not been eradicated.

He was to remain in New York three months; but his health continued so poor, and the prospect of his recovery seemed so remote, that his friends and the officials of the charge persuaded Mr. Rankin to extend the time indefinitely, lest a return to the malarious regions northward or westward might increase his distress. His three months' term was, therefore, extended to one of eight months. Credited to most other men, the itinerating and evangelizing done during these eight months would seem a miracle; but by him they were esteemed as barely worthy of being noted in his journal.

Maryland was the magnet of his heart during this season of distress and submission. There his friends were, and there he longed to be. Macedonian hands beckoned to him from the shore of every frith and bay. Importuning messages invited him to return, and that without delay. Influential people even offered to come and conduct him thither, in spite of discipline, if only he said the word; for the spirit of Strawbridge was abroad in the land.

At the end of the eight months Mr. Rankin requested him to proceed to Philadelphia. This he did, and remained in charge of that important post for three months—that is to say, from December 2, 1774, to February 22, 1775. At the end of that time he set out for Baltimore, possibly with the nominal consent of Rankin; but in reality, it would appear, as the result of his own choice and insistency. His stay in Baltimore at this time covered about sixty days; but he was much of the time inactive. Perhaps he was restrained by friends who saw his need of rest. His journal, however, shows that he held not a few meetings, that some of them were attended with signal manifestations of spiritual power, and that they were fruitful of results. His mind was at rest, and he was constantly refreshed with the fellowship of his friend Otterbein and with visits to "Perry Hall."

But even amid these agreeable surroundings there are evidences that the misunderstanding with Rankin was unreconciled. Before his departure from Philadelphia letters had gone from both his own and Rankin's hands to Mr. Wesley, though Asbury had been frank enough to read to his superior the statements and complaints which he was sending to England. A diplomatic silence obtained, and the Conference session was near at hand. Mr. Wesley would, no doubt, the next year have recalled Asbury to be near himself, or appointed him to service in the Bahamas; but a tragical and unforeseen providence prevented the removal from the New World of its destined apostle. The American Revolution was already a fact, and intercourse between the Mother Country and the Colonies was practically at an end.

CHAPTER VII.

Faith against Swords.

The Conference of 1775 met, as had those of the two previous years, in St. George's Church, Philadelphia. The day of opening—May 17—fell exactly one week later than the date of the opening of the second Continental Congress, which had convened in Liberty Hall. It is not likely that the patriots who sat in that first Capitol of the nation knew of the presence of a handful of lay preachers in conference so near their own chamber. The thoughts of the publicists were concerned with stamp acts, taxation, the rights of the Colonies, and the limitations of the royal government. War had not been declared against the mother country; but hostilities had already begun, the battle of Lexington having occurred in the preceding April. The land was filled with rumors of the coming strife, and the minds of the people were heavy with apprehensions.

The first war note found in Asbury's journal is in an entry made on April 30, 1775, twenty days before the meeting of the Conference. In this entry he says: "We have alarming military accounts from Boston, New York, and Philadelphia. Surely the Lord will overrule, and make these things subservient to the spiritual welfare of the Church." There were then no steam mail lines, no daily papers, no telegraphs, nor telephones. The news traveled slowly, and multiplied itself at each stage of advance. Boston Harbor and the foot of Bunker Hill were then the scenes of military activity. But Boston was a long way from the center of the Methodist world. Northern New Jersey, or perhaps Southern Connecticut, was at this time the farthest northward range of any of the itinerants. Amid the cry of tidings, some true, some exaggerated, "the preachers in connection with the Reverend John Wesley," many of whom were loyal British subjects, had ridden to their gathering in the city soon to become the birthplace of American liberty. The conditions were depressing to all, but to none more than to Rankin, who in his journal notes the effect upon the Conference.

But one, at least, of the British brethren was calm and undisturbed, whatever the prophecy conveyed to him by the disjointed times. That was Francis Asbury, who from the first seems to have made up his mind to stay with the Americans and share their fate. In all the entries in his journal which touch upon the war, he did not once betray a partisan spirit. Whether in England or in America, he had but one fealty, and that was to the kingdom of heaven. There, however, came a time when he felt, and could express, pride in being a citizen of the republic.

At the Conference a day of prayer and fasting was appointed for the prosperity of the work and for the peace of America. The year then closing had witnessed a great ingathering. Three thousand one hundred and forty-eight members in society were reported, and nineteen preachers were given appointments. Asbury was appointed to labor in Norfolk, Va. There were no signs of a renewal of the conflict of judgment between him and Rankin. Impressed, as they no doubt were, with the gravity of the experience through which the infant Church was clearly fore-doomed to pass, they laid aside their differences and worked together in a spirit of concession. It is probable, too, that the appointments were made after a very full discussion in open conference of the effect upon the work of the existing and threatened condition of public affairs. Rankin says in his journal: "We conversed together, and concluded our business in love. We wanted all the light and advice we could obtain respecting our conduct in the present critical situation of affairs."

The strained relations between Asbury and Rankin ended with this Conference, and there seems to have been much confidence and a real warmth of brotherly feeling between them from this time to the end of Rankin's stay in the country. No doubt Rankin came to a more correct appraisement of Asbury's ability, and Asbury, in turn, found that his superior was neither so obdurate nor so overbearing as he had at first suspected. It is the old story of human limitations within which the acts of even holy apostles have sometimes been found blameworthy.

Methodism was introduced into Norfolk and Portsmouth in 1772 by Robert Williams, an irregular Wesleyan preacher who preceded Boardman and Pilmoor to America by some months. He was one of the most interesting characters of the early Methodist era—zealous, impetuous, passionately religious, and rudely eloquent. His prophecy was burdened with a cry against the worldliness of the priests of the Established Church. He was an anti-hierarchical zealot, a republican, and the embodiment of gospel self-abnegation. And yet he was an enigma to the world and to his brethren. Ignorant of how to submit to discipline, he labored with marvelous results; utterly dead to the world, he yet understood beyond all the men of his fellowship how to use the world as not abusing it. He printed books, and sold them while sweeping around his wilderness circuits, and toward the end of his remarkable career he married, and left at his death an estate considerable enough to be administered upon. He was, as the history of the early itinerants goes, the first of the preachers to print a book, the first to marry, and the first to die. The supreme distinction of his life, however, is that of being the spiritual father of Jesse Lee, the apostle of Methodism to New England.

For a preaching place in Portsmouth Williams had secured a vacant store, and for a chapel in Norfolk an abandoned playhouse. He had also gathered a small society; but the population was obdurate, and no extraordinary headway had been made previous to the time of Asbury's coming,

From the miracles that had attended his ministry at Baltimore, at the Point, and amongst the plantations in Maryland, Asbury found himself transferred to conditions upon which even the fiery zeal of Williams had but feebly told. But he was nearing his thirtieth year, and to a rich experience was adding the judgment and mastery of maturity. To his difficult task he addressed himself with purpose.

The handful of members which he found in society were soon reduced a half by the application of discipline for which he always stood. This done, he began a characteristic move upon the adjacent coasts and the wide region westward and northward of the twin ports. His circuit covered the country lying between the Dismal Swamp and the great estuary, and as far northward as he had time and strength to ride. What had been difficult to Williams under happier conditions became all but impossible to Asbury, with the fever of war consuming the souls of the people. Politics and unbelief when mingled make a refractory composition. But the man of faith, hungering for holiness and peace and for human souls, went on with his work. Like a true captain, when the oppositions seemed strongest, he ordered an advance. A subscription for the building of a chapel was set on foot; but the utmost that could be secured was £34. How faint a prophecy that of the modern Methodist Norfolk, with its many and costly churches!

About midsummer of this year, Thomas Rankin for himself and others of the English preachers notified Asbury that on account of the growing enmity to loyal British subjects in the revolted provinces he judged it best for them to return at an early day to England. To this communication Asbury returned a prompt and vigorous answer to the effect that, whatever Rankin and others chose to do, he himself was determined to remain with the flock in America. This courageous stand of the former General Assistant caused Rankin to change his mind for the time. His departure from the continent was thus postponed for two years.

A notable revival had been in progress in Virginia prior to 1775. It had begun under the ministry of the Rev. Devereux Jarratt, a priest of the Established Church, who had affiliated with the Methodists and used their methods, even organizing societies for the training of converts. In 1773 Robert Williams joined himself to Jarratt, and the revival took on extraordinary proportions. Then came George Shadford, whom Wesley had sent to America with the commission to "publish his message in the face of the sun," and the pentecostal circle widened from district to district, and from county to county. Nothing like it had been seen in America before, and it was this awakening in Virginia which accounts for the extraordinary growth of the Methodist societies between 1775 and 1777. In fact, the impetus of it was felt in Methodism for half a hundred years later.

The Brunswick Circuit was the center of this noteworthy movement, and George Shadford was assistant in charge. In October, provided with a chaise, Asbury said farewell to Norfolk, and drove southward to Brunswick to join Shadford. Whether he went by appointment of Rankin or by invitation of Shadford does not appear. Bishop McTyeire describes his absence as a "vacation." If so, it was a vacation from which he never returned. The state of war had greatly interfered with an orderly administration of Conference affairs. Many of the preachers were under the necessity of becoming a law to themselves. This was particularly true of those itinerants in the coast cities exposed to invasion or bombardment. British marines had already landed at Norfolk, and soon after Asbury's departure the city was burned by order of the Tory governor of Virginia. Asbury had no immediate successor, and the circuit does not again appear in the list of appointments until 1777.

During the four succeeding months Asbury was within the revival circle in the interior. It was remote from the scenes of incipient war; the land was populous, the work of God was prospering as he desired it should in every place, and the soul of the visiting itinerant went out in a glow. He rode from revival to revival. At a certain quarterly meeting where he preached seven hundred people were reckoned to be present. This meeting licensed three preachers, who afterwards became distinguished in the history of Methodism. They were Francis Poythress, James Foster, and Joseph Hartley.

Some time after this Asbury visited the Rev. Mr. Jarratt, the evangelical Anglican who had been so largely instrumental in promoting the Virginia revival. The two held several meetings together, and for years afterwards they were united in the closest bonds of friendship and confidence. Some time later, when the societies and preachers were without proper superintendency on account of the long continuance of the war, they were by action of Conference recommended to seek advice of this godly and evangelical priest. Several of the early Methodist historians refer to him as "the American Fletcher," and the designation, in view of his spirit and zeal, is not inapt.

About this time a letter came from Rankin directing Asbury to repair to Philadelphia, and again assume charge of the societies in that war-troubled center. After giving some time to administering upon the will of his lately deceased fellow-itinerant, Robert Williams, he set off for Philadelphia by the way of Baltimore. For the next few months his journal constantly records rumors of an impending conflict. A great army was expected to arrive from England in the spring, and feverish preparation was being made by the colonies to resist. No conjecture could be risked as to where the chief attack would be delivered, and so every exposed community suffered from disturbing and distressing apprehensions.

To add to the distress of the work and the embarrassment of the preachers, Mr. Wesley's ill-advised "Calm Address to the American Colonies" had made its appearance. The immediate effect was to put the whole body of Methodists under the suspicion of disloyalty, and raise against the preachers, English and native, the cry of "Tory." The copies of the address sent to Rankin were summarily burned; but the interested Tory government found a way to smuggle others in. The confusion wrought by this pamphlet cannot be appreciated at this distance. Rankin read the logic of it, and at the Conference held that year left himself without an appointment, that he might be able to go generally over the field to allay suspicion and preach down resentment, or, if so extreme a need should arise, that he might be free to leave the country at a moment's notice.

The Conference met in Baltimore, in the newly opened Lovely Lane Chapel, on the 21st day of May, six weeks before the signing of the Declaration of Independence. Asbury was not at the Conference, having been seized on his way thither with a severe illness, a recrudescence of former malarial poisonings. Feeble but not despondent, he made his way back to Philadelphia, and awaited the return of his northern bound brethren to bring him news from the Conference.

Within a fraction of five thousand members were reported in society, and twenty-four preachers received

6

appointments. Amongst the names of those admitted on trial into the traveling connection appears that of Freeborn Garrettson, the avant-courier of early Methodism. Varied were the types of gifts, zeal, and heroism in the company of the itinerants that led the Wesleyan movement in North America; but of that immortal guard no name retains a surer luster nor begets a more certain inspiration than that of Freeborn Garrettson.

As in the previous year, the Conference finished its proceedings with a resolution appointing a day of fasting and prayer for the peace of America. In his sick chamber at Philadelphia, Asbury received the information that he had been appointed assistant in charge of the Baltimore work. This was his fourth assignment to that circuit. Beyond a doubt, the news was a solace to him. Weak and wasted with long and frequent sicknesses, he rode southward to that haven of rest and earthly happiness, "Perry Hall," where his friends, the Goughs, received him with tender affection and attended him with tireless ministries.

In returning to Maryland, he naturally felt that he was returning to his own; but a foretaste of the sore experience he was to pass through during the next few years awaited him. The new political order was asserting itself vigorously. Asbury had failed to take out a civil license as a preacher. For this neglect—perhaps he was wholly ignorant of the necessity of such license—he was arrested and fined ten pounds. The rule, an old and inoperative one, had been revived with a view to limiting the loyalist propensities of the priests of the State Church. The fact that

Asbury was an Englishman suggested to the colonial police the desirability of putting him under the rule.

After about three weeks of active work in Maryland, during which time he was more than once exposed to drenching rains, a malignant sore throat, the result of malarial poisoning long uncorrected, prostrated him, and brought him near to death. It was now decided by his friends, the Goughs and Dallams, that he must take a vacation—strange sound to him!—and go to the Warm Sulphur Springs in Virginia for his health, even for the saving of his life. It was midsummer, and the Goughs and Dallams were soon to go thither on their annual outing. Having made provision to supply his circuit, Asbury set forth with his friends on the journey to the Springs. "That no opportunity might be lost," sick and shattered in frame though he was, he "ventured to preach" twice in Baltimore, and at night in the tavern at which he stopped the second day out. A great company was found at the Springs—a field white unto harvest, as he fondly hoped—and so he arranged a meeting each evening for preaching and exhortation in the cottage of Mr. Gough, or in some others that he found open. In addition to this, he preached three times each week and once on the Sabbath in the open air. At this time also his daily reading did not fall short of the accustomed one hundred pages. A task this for an invalid! And yet to him it was rest, soul-restoring rest. Moreover, his health improved steadily; nor was he without a variety of instructive and edifying experiences outside of his routine. He met not a few of such people as are usually attracted to such a resort—people of means, leisure, and intelligence of a sort, but possessed of freakish religious notions. He describes with some severity two spiritless sermons which he heard, and a conversation which he had with an antinomian. Serious man that he was, he had a keen sense of the ridiculous, and was quick to detect a sham; nor was he slow to expose it—at least in his journal.

After six weeks of active resting at the Springs, with reinvigorated blood and fiber, he was back in Maryland, preaching to great crowds at many of the rural stations, and witnessing a general ingathering of converts. The results of the year for all Maryland were, in round numbers, little short of one thousand additions to the members in society. Constant tidings of the continued revival in Virginia also cheered him and his fellow-workers. The evangelism of the period was contagious: a wave of spiritual power seemed to be steadily rising in the two Colonies. With these tokens about him, and with constant access to his confiding and helpful friend Otterbein, there was now but one thing to give Asbury heaviness, and that was the ever deepening cloud of war that hung about the land.

Near the end of February, leaving Joseph Hartley in charge of the Baltimore stations, he rode through blinding snows to open a new work in Annapolis, the capital. The new State assembly was in session, flushed with the pride of recently declared independence, and confident in the thought of nationality. The town was notoriously irreligious, being a hotbed of typical eighteenth century deism. The young itinerant aimed at nothing short of the evangelization of this place. It was a Herculean undertaking; but it was a spiritual Hercules who undertook it. Eventually not a few of the members of the assembly attended upon his ministry. By the middle of spring a pronounced impression had been made upon the whole body of the people. When he delivered his last sermon preparatory to reporting to the Conference, a notable congregation waited upon his message and importuned him to return.

CHAPTER VIII.

A Mastery of Spirits.

WE now come to sketch the history of a series of events that tested Asbury's spirit and brought out his powers of mastery and leadership. But for the distinct and crucial situation created by these events, it is doubtful if the providential mission of Asbury to the New World could have been so completely and effectively realized as it was.

The Conference of 1777 met in a country chapel at Deer Creek, in Harford County, Maryland, on the twentieth day of May. Asbury and certain other members of the Conference held an unofficial preliminary meeting at "Perry Hall," the home of the Goughs, at which the stationing of the preachers and other matters were discussed. Two important departures were proposed. One was a plan to have Rankin administer the ordinances; but this was summarily voted down. Another was that, in view of the almost certain early departure of Rankin, and possibly of the other English preachers, a committee of American preachers should be appointed to superintend the societies when it should happen that no General Assistant was on the ground. This was favorably considered, and the committee was regularly appointed by the Conference. No account of this action appears in the printed minutes of the year; but a contemporaneous document supplies the record, and also gives the names of the members of the committee. They were: William Watters, Philip Gatch, Daniel Ruff, Edward Dromgoole, and William Glendenning.

Thomas Rankin was present, and presided; though he announced that both he and the other English brethren would soon take their departure for the mother country. For their use and protection certificates of character were issued by the Conference. But this did not include the name of Asbury, for he had already announced his purpose to remain with the Americans. Nevertheless, his recall by Wesley had not been revoked, and it was foreseen that the order to return might be renewed at any time.

The American brethren urged that those English preachers who had been demitted should remain to the last moment. Accordingly George Shadford and Martin Rodda were given appointments, the one in Maryland and the other in Delaware. Rankin, as in the two previous years, gave himself no assignment; neither does the name of Asbury appear in the station list. However, immediately after the Conference he rode to Annapolis, and took up the work which he had left but a few weeks before, and which had become a part of the Baltimore Circuit.

The absence of Asbury's name from the list of appointments for this year has been a puzzle to the historians; but to me the explanation is on the face of things. Rankin, expecting to leave the country at any time, arranged with Asbury, with whom he had come to an understanding, to take up the superintendency of the societies the moment he should depart. This only can explain why Asbury's name did not head the provisional committee. So long as Asbury should be on the ground the commission plan was inoperative. Proof of this will appear later.

The line of travel which Asbury laid out for himself indicates that he had already been admitted by Rankin to a joint superintendency, which was to become complete the moment Rankin took ship. This will also explain the frequent meetings of Asbury and Rankin during the remaining weeks of the latter's stay. It seems, too, that in August Asbury insisted on Rankin's taking a three months' service in Baltimore. This suggestion could not have been made with any degree of seemliness unless some understanding had been on between them. Rankin had his reasons for declining to go to Baltimore; but they were not a denial of the right of Asbury to suggest the appointment. Within a month Rankin was on the high seas bound for England.

Asbury now manifested the sign of a General Assistant by widening his circuit. In a little while it included the greater part of Maryland, and he was on the point of extending his oversight to other parts of the field when he learned that George Shadford, the last of the English preachers besides himself, had embarked for Europe. This left the Baltimore Circuit in a state of crying need. There was no course open to Asbury but to remain in Maryland and supply the lack. This he was proceeding to do when the Maryland officers informed him that he must take the oath of allegiance to the new State government. The punishment for failure to do so was extradition or imprisonment. Maryland did not accept the Articles of Federation until 1781; but from the first she demanded a strict loyalty from those within her borders. Asbury declined to naturalize. As a loyal Englishman, he could not, and as a minister his conscience was against the oath. As a means of personal safety, he repaired to the State of Delaware, where no such oath was required, and where he hoped to live in peace as a nonjuror. In this he was mistaken, and of course his work as General Assistant was over until conditions changed.

In Delaware he found an asylum in the hospitable home of Judge White, of the Kent County Court of Common Pleas, who, though a High-churchman, had long been a friend and admirer of the faithful evangelist. The White home came to be to him a place only second in his affections to "Perry Hall." Here he was in practical exile for many months, though he managed to sally forth and preach in a nine days' circuit about the castle of his protector. He also held frequent meetings in the barn on the White estate, and it was in this same barn that he organized the movement which no doubt changed the whole history of early American Methodism, and marked him as a man of marvelous foresight and leadership, such leadership, however, as answers to no rule in books of military tactics and contradicts every precedent developed in the stories of the mighty. This man who walked by faith led his fellows captive by the same rule.

Although he finally escaped bodily harm, or arrest, he suffered not a few persecutions, and was often in imminent danger from those who counted him an enemy of their country. He saw his noble host arrested and dragged away to prison, perhaps for his sake, and he was himself compelled to hide for a considerable time in a neighboring swamp to escape the hands of those who meant him evil.

Others of the itinerants were not so fortunate. Several were imprisoned at Annapolis by the Maryland police. Hartley was beaten and cast into a dungeon. Freeborn Garrettson was not only confined in jail, but was assaulted by a petty ex-judge and felled from his horse. Peddicord was brutally assaulted, and received wounds the scars of which he carried to his grave; and yet another member of the Conference lost an eye because of his zeal for the Word.

They suffered under the false accusation of being Tories and sympathizers with royalty. This came to them because of Mr. Wesley's unwise pamphlet on the stamp act and the war. But notwithstanding all they suffered, not one was silenced or forgot that he served the Lord Christ.

The test of Methodism was now at hand. The Conference of 1778 met in Leesburg, Va. Of course Asbury did not preside. He could not even be present, it being impossible for him to cross the territory of Maryland, and indeed dangerous for him to venture far from the home of his protector.

William Watters, the first named of the provisional committee appointed the previous year and the first native American admitted into the traveling connection, presided over the deliberations of the Conference. Amongst those admitted on trial at Leesburg was James O'Kelley, a man of whom we shall have occasion to speak again as this narrative progresses.

At the Conference held at Deer Creek, the last over which Rankin presided, it had been resolved to lay the whole matter of the ordinances "over for the determi-

nation of the Conference to be held at Leesburg."
But still so uncertain were these lay itinerants of the
ground upon which their issue was pitched that they
again deferred action to the session of the Conference
to be held the succeeding year in Fluvanna County,
Virginia. It is more than probable that this post-
ponement was secured by Watters himself. His con-
servatism nearly approached that of the English
preachers, and in the succeeding year he allied himself
with Asbury, and assisted in the defeat of the sacramental party.

The Leesburg minutes make no mention of Asbury's
name. His enforced inactivity put him in the rank
of a local preacher. The name of William Watters
leads the list of assistants, and this made him the *de
facto* head of the societies. In consequence of the
war, the numbers in society had fallen off nearly one
thousand, and the number of preachers had been considerably reduced. This was one of the few years
in the history of American Methodism in which there
has been recorded an actual loss.

Though the Conference adjourned, leaving the sacramental question where it had rested for a year, it
soon began to be apparent that sentiment upon the
subject was advancing. Watters and other conserva-
tives saw that radical action would be taken at the
Conference to be held in 1779. Whether or not they
communicated their fears to Asbury cannot now be
stated with certainty. But though remote from the
scene, and in exile, Asbury gathered accurate information concerning the course of events, and deeply meditated a plan for circumventing what had now passed
beyond the ordinary means of correction.

In the meantime Asbury was not idle as an itinerant, though without an appointment. Freeborn Garrettson, who was assistant on the Delaware Circuit, divided the work with him, and in all matters deferred to him as though he were the superior by appointment. He dared not go beyond the borders of Delaware; but was constantly visited by former comrades, and he kept his eye on the work from Pennsylvania to Virginia. His influence and the respect in which he was held were but little, if any, diminished by his long isolation. In fact, during this year his ascendency over the preachers of "the Northern stations" became complete. His sufferings, his zeal, and the unexampled power of his ministry as a "prisoner of Jesus Christ" were known and testified to all along the western shore. In some way it was read by many that to him had been committed the book of the law and the leadership of the hosts to be. All those preachers under his immediate shadow were won away from the desire to break with Mr. Wesley and take up the administration of the sacraments. Those farther away from him—namely, all those in Virginia which now contained, with the stations in North Carolina, far more than half of all the members in society, as also a substantial majority of the preachers—were determined to follow the example of Strawbridge and administer the ordinances on the ground that providence had supplied the necessary grant of authority.

Foreseeing the course of the preachers in the South, Asbury called a Conference of those itinerants stationed north of the Virginia line. He had seen the advantage of a before-Conference caucus in 1777, and he no doubt at first meant that this meeting should be nothing more than such. But, like Mr. Wesley, when he found that one wise step logically called for another, that other was taken without hesitancy. The plan for a caucus matured into a call for a Conference. The session was held in the barn on the Judge White estate, in Kent County, Delaware, April 28, 1777, exactly three weeks before the date appointed for the meeting of the regular Conference in Fluvanna County, Virginia.

Several reasons have been assigned for the calling of this "little Conference," or *"quasi* Conference," as it has been styled by different historians. The most apparent was that Asbury could not attend the regular session held beyond the borders of Delaware. But a reason given by Asbury himself was that the Northern brethren might be prepared for the regular session, which is perhaps a franker reason than even honest Asbury meant to state. So well were these brethren prepared for the regular Conference that practically none of them attended its sittings. The real reason for holding this Northern Conference was one of masterful strategy—namely, to prevent a separation of the societies from Mr. Wesley and to defeat the sacramental party. The Virginia Conference was regular; the Delaware Conference was irregular. When that is said, the constitutional question has been exhausted. Some historians have referred to the Virginians as schismatics. That is an anachronism of prejudice. Asbury's Conference can be justified only by the logic of successful revolution. It was the self-vindicating expedient of a seer and a master of men.

Sixteen preachers constituted the Delaware Conference. They agreed to acknowledge the authority of

Asbury as General Assistant, accept the appointments made by him, and remain in connection with Mr. Wesley. William Watters, the head of the Governing Committee appointed in 1777, and who had presided at Leesburg, rode from his station in Northern Virginia to attend this Conference and to urge Asbury to attend the regular session in Virginia. That he had been privy to Asbury's plans is proved by the fact that he took an appoinment to Baltimore, and thus formally separated himself from his colleagues in the South. "A soft and healing epistle" was written the Virginians begging them to desist from their contemplated course. This epistle rested the case for a year.

Thus fortified with an organized Conference behind him, and with his authority as Mr. Wesley's legate revived, Asbury awaited the issue of events.

The regular Conference met at the appointed time. William Watters was present, but did not preside. That responsibility fell to Philip Gatch, whose name stood second on the Governing Committee. The Conference promptly entered upon a policy of independency, and resolved to constitute a presbytery for the decent ordination of a ministry. This presbytery consisted of three members, with Philip Gatch at its head. The members were authorized to administer the sacraments and to convey by ordination a like authority to others whom they deemed worthy.

The war of the Revolution had now reached its most tragic stage. Direct communication with England had long been at an end. The spiritual destitution of the country was great; the priests of the Established Church had nearly all deserted their cures. The preachers in the Virginia Conference were, without exception, Americans. The call to do what they did seemed imperative. They were the children of gospel expediency, and they followed the law of their being.

By the action of the Conference the societies were erected into a Presbyterian Church. The breach with the Northern Conference was thus, to all appearances, complete. Satisfied with what they had done, the Virginia itinerants went forth to their societies, suddenly raised to the status of Christian Churches, and began to baptize their converts and give to their congregations the bread and wine of the Holy Supper.

The wrongness of this course was wholly in its inexpediency. It was legal, it was canonical, it was scriptural; but it was a course unadvisedly taken. The time selected was not that appointed of providence. It failed in the end, and failed logically.

The people received the ordinances gladly; and in the face of the fact that the war was at its tragic height, the revival in Virginia continued. The increase in membership in these parts during a period beginning with January, 1779, was phenomenal. Not unnaturally these tokens were accepted by both preachers and people as an indorsement by Providence of the sacramental departure.

Asbury passed the remainder of the year in great activity. In study and travel he fairly eclipsed his former record, though his circuit lay wholly within the State of Delaware. His condition, too, was now much ameliorated. New and strong friends had come to his aid, amongst them the Governor of Delaware, under whose protection he had placed himself. He had also found in Delaware another "American Fletcher" in the person of the Rev. Mr. McGraw, of the Established Church, who, like Jarratt, had aligned himself with the Methodists and became their defender. A continuous revival went on here as well, and the number of communicants in the Church greatly increased, for the Delaware Methodists considered themselves Episcopalians.

Asbury constantly indulged the hope that the Southern societies would, at the end of the year, make overtures for an agreement and union with the societies in the North. This hope came of his own knowledge of the preachers, and was stimulated by letters which he received from individual itinerants in the South. Events showed that he had not wholly mistaken his brethren; but the task of reconciliation proved greater than he calculated.

The Northern Conference had adjourned to meet in Baltimore April 25, 1780. Asbury rode thither, crossing over to Maryland soil for the first time in more than two years. A passport from the Governor of Delaware secured him safe conduct; but in Maryland he was a nonjuror, and could not preach. His presidency over the Conference was not interdicted; but as a prophet or a minister he dared not speak. Under this constrained "silence" his spirit chafed; but it was a consequence of war.

As had been anticipated, a letter came from the Virginia Methodists. This letter was delivered by messengers empowered to treat. Several proposals were made by Asbury, but were rejected by the messengers. At last Asbury suggested a suspension of the administration of the ordinances for one year, and an appeal to Wesley, with union and coöperation in the meantime. The messengers thought this might do, and agreed to bear the offer to their brethren. Asbury, Garrettson, and Watters were appointed to visit the Virginians as commissioners from the Northern body.

The Southern Conference was to meet at Broken-back Church, Manikintown, Va., May 9, 1780. In company with Garrettson and Watters, Asbury started thither about the first of May. Having perfected his American citizenship papers, he had the great joy during his southward journey to preach to his former parishioners in Baltimore. In due time he and his fellow-commissioners arrived at the seat of the Virginia Conference.

Being invited to come before the Conference, Asbury read Mr. Wesley's thoughts against separation from the Church of England, together with a letter received by him at some earlier date from Mr. Wesley on the same subject. He also discussed the proposals made to the Southern messengers at Baltimore two weeks before. He did not speak forensically, or in the spirit of demand, but in tones of persuasiveness and love. The effect of his address was so nearly a healing of the difference that the preachers agreed to suspend the administrations on the ground that Asbury should supply the ordinances to the circuits. This, however, he could not do; and so the matter rested for the time.

Asbury closed the morning session of the Conference with a sermon which melted many hearts. The way to an understanding seemed to have opened afresh; but at the afternoon session the prospect had departed. Asbury then renewed the proposal to suspend the administrations pending an appeal to Wesley,

7

after which he and his companions withdrew that the Conference might have freedom of discussion. Repairing to his lodgings near by, Asbury fell upon his face in prayer. It was an hour of agony and loud crying for the healing of the hurt of Zion. The hour having expired, the commissioners were recalled to receive the answer of the Conference. The terms of union could not be accepted. The close of negotiations was abrupt enough.

The commissioners now prepared to return to their stations in the North. Asbury went again to his lodgings to take final leave of his host; but once more in his chamber, he fell upon his face and prayed "as with a broken heart." Earthly help was gone; but the man of many and mighty prayers laid hold upon the feet of Power. Mounting his horse, he rode away; but alighted at the place where the Conference was being held to say farewell to those who had chosen to reject his counsel. What was his joy and surprise, if a man of such faith as his could be surprised of Heaven, to find that while he and his companions had been praying the Conference had accepted his terms. The administration of the ordinances was to be suspended, and there was to be but one Conference. "Surely the hand of God has been greatly seen in all this" was the calmly grateful speech which Asbury indulged in reflecting on the fruitful end of his labors and prayers.

To consummate the act of union, the commissioners were seated in the Conference. Asbury assumed the chair, and stationed the preachers. He was also requested by Conference action to take general oversight of the work and communicate with Mr. Wesley in the name of the reunited societies.

CHAPTER IX.

THE NEW AMERICAN.

WITH the happy close of the Conference in Virginia, in 1780, dawned not only a new era for Methodism in America, but a new civic experience came to its leader. From that hour Asbury began to be an American. Having been made a full citizen in Delaware some days before, he was now free to go as he chose. The invitation of the Virginians to ride through their territory was therefore accepted, and the task entered upon without delay.

The gloomiest days of the war were at hand. Cornwallis had overrun South Carolina and was pressing northward to a strong position at Camden, where he later inflicted a crushing defeat on the Americans under General Gates. A division of the Continental army was now moving southward, and Asbury was sometimes in its wake, sometimes on its flank, as he stopped to preach, and then rode a forced stage to meet another waiting company. There was daily expectation of hostilities at the front, but in the face of these threatening conditions the tireless itinerant pressed on through southern Virginia and upper North Carolina, the stages of his journey aggregating more than a thousand miles marked by literally hundreds of sermons and exhortations.

Asbury was now bishop *de facto*. The whole work had been put under his care by competent canonical action. He had been given by the Northern Conference primacy in all matters of administration and the

same power over legislation as that enjoyed by Mr.
Wesley in England, and this had been practically
agreed to by the preachers in the South. But for all
this there was much to do to perfectly heal the breach
made by the sacramental controversy. There were
members of the party of separation yet to be met and
reconciled; a questioning spirit amongst the people
had also to be answered. This was one of the chief
ends to be served by the tour. Therefore as he advanced he not only called sinners to repentance, but
gently urged the saints to be of one mind. Methodists
he exhorted to follow him as he followed Wesley. Relief was sure to come at no distant day, and they must
be patient.

This work of reconciliation was not easy. The Established Church had collapsed, and, except in a few
cases, its priests had either fled or had been expelled
from the country. The people were receiving with
gladness the old-new truths of the gospel as preached
by the Methodists, and they demanded that these truths
should be confirmed in the sacraments. With mon-
archy they had given up sacerdotalism, and could not
understand why the administrations had been suspended. But such was his power over men of all stations
that wherever Asbury went these doubts were composed, though elsewhere much unrest continued to prevail. He had, however, set himself to silence the controversy, and could neither withhold his voice nor rest
his goings until he saw the end.

In Virginia he had the joy to meet again the Rev.
Mr. Jarratt, who was one of the few priests of the
Establishment remaining in the country. Being a
native of Virginia and in full sympathy from the first

7935

with the efforts of the colonies to gain their independence, he was naturally a man much respected, while his evangelical spirit and his zeal as a preacher made him doubly a light in the darkness of his times. He undertook to assist Asbury in composing the differences in the societies, and agreed to attend and participate in the proceedings of the forthcoming Methodist Conference.

It was during this tour also that Asbury had his first meeting with James O'Kelley, who afterwards became his strong antagonist, and led the first schism from the Methodist body in America. The impression which the future schismatic made upon the future bishop was most favorable, and for a long time after this meeting there was much confidence between them. Indeed, O'Kelley now stood next to the leader himself.

About this time Asbury was joined by Edward Bailey, a faithful local preacher, who became his traveling companion on the journey through North Carolina. In a chaise they traversed the wide and unmarked circuits, fording deep rivers, winding and cutting their way through trackless forests and over broken and rocky ledges. Crossing the Tar, the Neuse, and the Haw Rivers, they pushed well-nigh into the heart of the State. Returning by a more westerly path, they came to the town of Hillsboro, then a place of some importance, and still possessing a real historic interest. From this point they continued their return in a direct course to the Virginia line, and on the 8th of September crossed the Roanoke River, having spent somewhat more than two months in the Carolina Circuits. Soon after returning to Virginia Asbury was deeply saddened by the death of his faithful traveling companion, who expired, after a brief warning, in the midst of zealous labors.

About this time also he took another degree in patriotism, and was led to more fully declare his fealty to the American cause. On receipt of the news that the army of General Gates had been defeated by Cornwallis, he wrote in his journal: "I have a natural affection for my own countrymen; yet I can hear them called cruel, and calmly listen to threatenings of slaughter against them." It was his sense of English justice that made him a loyal American.

Although the Virginia Conference had adjourned early in May, it was not until the middle of September that Asbury communicated to Mr. Wesley information of the reconciliation of the divided societies. There are two possible reasons for this delay. The first is that Asbury may have found no earlier opportunity for dispatching a letter. Private postal matter meant for England had first to go either to France or the Netherlands, and from thence through the post of another and friendly power. Ships sailed at long and uncertain intervals. But what is more likely to have been the reason was that Asbury desired first to satisfy himself as to the sentiment amongst the people. The contents of the letter which he wrote are not now fully known, but the communication which came from Mr. Wesley by the hand of Dr. Coke in 1784 and the commission which he bore to organize a Church and ordain a clergy were a full answer to the request which it preferred.

From this first general tour Asbury returned to his earthly Eden, "Perry Hall," praying as he went a ceaseless prayer for the peace of the people he had seen scattered through the wilderness. His faith was strong, divinely strong; but he could not then grasp that vision of the future which would have given him rest from every thought of the morrow. But the ways of the Most High are hidden that the faith of his chosen may have its needed exercise.

At his going out in the early spring his purse had been by the princely Gough replenished with three guineas. This stock he had largely expended on his journey through the South; but the last farthing had gone from his hand only when he was in sight, as it were, of the gables of "Perry Hall." Thus the expenses incurred during nearly twice a thousand miles of travel were accounted for in the expenditure of somewhat less than ten dollars in coin and a few dollars of almost worthless Continental paper. It is not a matter of surprise that to a man of such simplicity and frugality a yearly salary of sixty-five dollars should seem an abundance!

The return of the General Assistant to the North was timely. During his half year of absence in Virginia trouble had arisen in Maryland and Delaware. The quarterly meetings had come on, and the exchange of preachers had taken place. With no authority present to arbitrate their differences of judgment, serious friction had resulted. This was the really weak point in the polity of early Methodism, but one which was afterwards remedied in the office of the presiding eldership.

Within a year after his new investiture Asbury saw the magnitude of his task. He must be constructively present in every part of the field. To make this possible he must cause his face and personality to become familiar to the whole body of the people called Methodists. The task was a large one. His apostleship had developed in a call to increased travel and labors; but the prospect gave him joy, and he shrank from no responsibility. He reëntered Delaware in November, and by the coming of New Year's Day all friction had been removed. Even graver difficulties yielded to his wise and gentle tactics. Letters came from Virginia saying: "The jarring string has been broken, and those who were friends at first are friends at last." The vision of the prophet upon Shiggionoth was repeated.

The advantage which came of holding two Conferences in 1779 and 1780 suggested to Asbury a continuance of the plan. Two sessions would accommodate a greater number of the preachers, and in the event of a renewal of the sacramental question or the emergence of a new difficulty, one section could be held as a check on the other. The point was not to be overlooked by so wise a leader and so careful a disciplinarian as Asbury. Two sittings were accordingly planned for 1781, the first to be had at Choptank, in Delaware, on April 16, and the other at Baltimore on April 24. This last sitting was, in fact, the regularly adjourned session of the Virginia Conference, which had met at Manikintown the previous year.

The statistics for the year showed ten thousand five hundred and ninety-four members in society and fifty-four preachers. At the Baltimore session there was for the first time in two years an attendance of preachers from the whole field and a healthy exchange of assistants and helpers between the North and the South. Asbury's remedy for schism, as also his rule of evangelism, was "a circulation of the preachers."

At this time a vast new missionary field was being opened up in the mountains of Northern Virginia, and to this territory the General Assistant rode after the session of the Conference. Setting out about the end of May, he pushed as far westward as Martinsburg. Turning northwestward from that point, he preached in the wild and picturesque mountain valleys along and beyond the south branch of the Potomac. There he longed to be able to speak with tongues that he might preach the gospel to the peoples and kindreds who had come to make their homes in those fair new lands. Commissioning men, he sent them forth to press beyond the mountains to the north and west and become the vanguard of an itinerant army that later brought the far-reaching valleys of the Ohio and its tributaries under the dominion of Methodism. In those wonder-spelling mountains he saw the gushing springs and explored the stalactite caves that have since made famous the Appalachian highlands of Virginia.

It was on this journey also that he had his first taste of real pioneering. On the bare floors of squatters' cabins, on the tops of naked chests, and even on the stony floor of mountain paths he found often his only rest for the night. But naturally he improved in bodily frame, breathing the ozone of those freer altitudes and drinking the uninfected waters filtered from mountain sands. At the end of the summer, with the fragrance of the laurel and the pine on his garments, high in spirits and with a widened vision of his undisputed see, he returned for a brief official tour of Maryland and Pennsylvania.

Letters from the Peninsula and from the lower stations in Virginia awaited him. Those from the Peninsula told of peace and continued revival. The priests of the expiring Establishment united with the Methodist exhorters in the call to repentance. Rev. Charles Pettigrew, an Anglican, afterwards elected to the Protestant Episcopal diocese of Delaware, was in warm sympathy with the revival. Freeborn Garrettson, lately released from prison, where he had suffered for the gospel's sake, had fired the workers with new zeal. Not the common people only, but the aristocracy, heard the message gladly. Now could Asbury see the meaning of his two years of exile in pent-up Delaware. The seed which he sowed during those months of seeming vanity had already begun to yield their fruit.

The letters from Virginia told of a no less advancing work; but there was still a note of discord—a sporadic discontent on account of the suspended ordinances. That meant another tour through those parts before the Conference should meet. But important as was that visit, it must be delayed. Philadelphia and the more northern stations, lately freed from the incubus of garrisoning armies, must be counseled and helped. The war had left in those parts many wastes that must be repaired without delay.

Now for the first time we begin to hear of "quarterly meeting Conferences;" and indeed at this time it is difficult to determine the line of distinction between the functions of a quarterly and an annual Conference. At the lesser, as at the greater, gathering Asbury organized circuits, appointed preachers, and administered discipline. Throughout there was no fixed program, but all things took the course of Christian expediency. The outlines of a great ecclesiasticism were, however, slowly coming into view.

No complete account of the Methodist movement in America had been written up to this time, and the need for such a narrative was being felt. Asbury undertook to supply the lack. This work must have been a mere pamphlet, and so far as I have been able to ascertain no copy of it is in existence. Of similar character was a brochure on the cause and cure of Church divisions, meant to offset the arguments of the Fluvanna party. Aside from his journal these appear to be the most serious literary essays he ever set himself to produce.

The Quarterly Conference visitations in the North being completed, he was again, at the beginning of winter, in Virginia. The point of going out was Bohemia Manor, the gateway through which he passed to that mysterious Southland that lay before him in the autumn of 1772. What miracles had been wrought in those ten years! When he first saw Bohemia Manor he was young and inexperienced; and though of a courageous faith, he was going forth as one not knowing whither he was led. Then the Methodists in America were but a few hundred; now they were thousands on thousands, and multiplying daily. Then he was the distrusted superior of half a dozen fellow-workers; now he was the chosen leader of threescore men of faith and iron, who were ready to go and come as he said, only asking that he follow Christ as they followed him.

Again his path led through that region of the Old Dominion where six years before so remarkable a revival had attended the labors of Shadford and Jarratt. There was there now a strong and growing Methodist constituency. The war had not affected the prosperity of the region, but it had been the center of the sacramental disturbance, and the general assistant approached it with apprehension. His fears were, however, groundless, for on arriving he found that the spirit of division was dead, or only lingered in fitful and widely separated manifestations.

All along Asbury had trusted much to the sympathy and good influence of Jarratt. Both the preachers and the people in Virginia had great respect for him, and were much influenced by his advice. This Virginia journey brought Asbury again into his home and parish. The fact that the initial sitting of the Conference for the year was to be had at Ellis's Preaching House in Sussex made it possible for Jarratt to redeem his pledge, made to Asbury the year before, to attend and participate. The sitting took place on April 17, and Mr. Jarratt opened the proceedings with a discourse. The preachers present signed a paper renewing the agreement of the former year concerning the sacraments, and the Conference closed with a second discourse by Mr. Jarratt. "The power of God was manifested in a most extraordinary manner," wrote Asbury in his journal the next day; "the preachers and people wept, believed, loved, and obeyed."

The Church priest and the Methodist general assistant then rode away together, but soon to separate, the Churchman to visit certain Virginia circuits as an evangelist, and the general assistant to look after distant parts of the field. As he continued his journey northward, he heard the welcome news that the war of the Revolution had ended in victory for the Colonies. His Americanism is reflected in this entry made the same day in his journal: "Here I heard the good news that Britain had acknowledged the independence for which America has been contending. May it be so!"

The Baltimore sitting of the Conference began on May 20. Since the minutes of both sittings were consolidated into one record, it is difficult to ascertain at which sitting any particular action began. It is understood, though, that important items went before each body for ratification. The minutes of the year show these actions to have been taken, originating, presumably, with the Virginians:

"Question 18. Shall we erase that question proposed in the Deer Creek Conference respecting the ordinances?"

"Answer. Undoubtedly we must; it can have no place in our minutes while we stand to our agreement signed in Conference; it is therefore disannulled."

"Ques. 19. Do the brethren in Conference choose Brother Asbury to act according to Mr. Wesley's original appointment, and preside over the American Conference and the whole work?"

"Ans. Yes."

Thus was the latter state of the unmitered Bishop made more secure than the first, and also was the desire of the people to have the ordinances at the hands of their own preachers sepulchered to have a triumphant resurrection in the Christmas Conference.

The latter half of 1782 was spent by Asbury in Maryland, Pennsylvania, and Delaware. His first care was to discharge a long-accumulating correspondence and look after certain Church properties embarrassed by ante-war debts. Another office was to plan relief for those chapels harassed by exorbitant ground rents,

a burdensome entailment of some of our present-day
Churches in Baltimore and other Eastern cities.

The New Year brought another call to Virginia.
His first sermon in the State was at Williamsburg, the
Colonial Capital, where the fiery eloquence of Patrick
Henry had stirred the Cavaliers in their first real re-
sistance to the Hanoverian tyrant. But when Asbury
saw it glory it had none. The functions and the func-
tionaries of State had long before removed to Richmond, and the preacher left it with little hope that it
would ever become a fruitful part of the spiritual vine-
yard.

Passing through Virginia, he again entered North
Carolina, pushing many leagues farther westward than
in 1780. The borders of Methodism had been extended
far beyond the Yadkin, even to the western base of
those uplooming mountains that then formed the hin-
terland of American civilization. Salem, the famous
Moravian settlement in the northern Piedmont, and
Hillsboro, the latter still suffering from the calamities
of war, were visited, as were many other intervening
points.

The Virginia sitting of the Conference recurred at
Ellis's Preaching House, in Sussex County, May 6,
1783. This session, as also the one which met twenty-
one days later in Baltimore, was conducted in great
peace. The question of African slavery, often referred
to by Asbury and more than once brought before the
Conference, came up in a more pronounced form than
it had hitherto assumed. The recently published peace
and the settled nationality of the Colonies gave to the
subject a new significance. "We all agreed in the
spirit of African liberty," wrote Asbury in his journal;

and a rule was made which required local as well as traveling preachers to manumit their slaves where the laws of the State permitted it.

The Conference of 1783 is chiefly famous as the one at which Jesse Lee was received on trial into the traveling connection. Few men were more active and prominent in the early American Church. As the first historian of Methodism and as the founder of the stations in New England, he has become known to later generations. Witty, eloquent, of commanding personality, and filled with the Holy Ghost, he was perhaps the most effective man in the itinerant ranks in his day. He barely missed election to the episcopacy in 1800; and it was he who as early as 1791 first sketched a plan for a delegated General Conference. This was seventeen years before Soule drafted the Constitution of Methodism. Lee and Asbury were strikingly unlike in mold and temperament, but they were able to cooperate in many great enterprises; yet, alas! too often their differences of mold and temperament caused unhappy misunderstandings to arise between them.

Asbury's circuit widened each year until it reached the limit of possible movement in that primitive time. Judging from his journal, however, the year between the Conferences of 1783 and those of 1784 seems to have been an exception; nevertheless, he covered much the same ground in Virginia and Carolina as he had in the previous year, and but for an ulcerated foot he would have crossed the mountains into the lands of the Holston. He had previously visited the stations in the North, including New York, from which he had been absent for several years, and which had been without a preacher during the British occupation. A

few months prior to his visit John Dickins had been
sent thither to renew the work.

Coming events were now casting distinct shadows.
A letter came to Asbury from Mr. Wesley in December appointing him to be General Assistant, a position
which he had been filling by election of his brethren
since 1780. Either through this letter or other medium
intimation had been given of Mr. Wesley's maturing
plans. It was known that he was asking ordination for
his preachers at the hands of the bishops of the Establishment. Indeed, the dénoument of the Christmas
Conference would no doubt have occurred in 1782 except for the refusal of the Anglican prelates to lay
hands on the diplomaless Methodists. Thus the secret
of the failure of Methodism to remain an adjunct of
the Anglican Church was a matter of Greek roots and
sheepskins. A mess of pottage changed the history
of the ancient world, and made the Jewish Church
possible. Providence is wiser than men.

The Conference met in the spring of 1784 in the confident belief that the deliverance of the long-distressed
societies was near at hand. Mr. Wesley's letter was
laid before the two sittings, and "all were happy." The
Conference was now united, compact, and dominated
by a spirit of absolute devotion. The members have
been described as men "dead to the world" and gifted
and enterprising in the things of God. The number
of members reported in society lacked but a round
dozen of being fifteen thousand, with ninety-three itinerant preachers. This Conference practically closed
the Colonial period of American Methodism. The
history-making Christmas Conference was but seven
months off.

CHAPTER X.

An Apostle by Proof.

THE careful student may discover in the destiny-used men of all times a quality of personality which suggests a truer philosophical basis of history than do the data arranged by either Buckle or Guizot. That quality is the ability of the actor in history not only to see the supreme opportunity when it is presented, but to rise to the height of its tests and requirements. This was the quality of Francis Asbury that stood him in the stead of genius. His sincerity of purpose and instant preparation of life were something more than the fruit of even religious loyalty. They were the manifestation of the spirit of history, the answer to the intelligent ordering and execution of the plans of Providence. The doctrine of immanences would be a contradiction, an absurdity, if it could not vindicate itself in this way.

Asbury had been slowly prepared for the supreme exigency of his life. Destiny was bound up in him, and the time was fast approaching. The Christmas Conference, of which as yet no Methodist in Europe or America had dreamed, was about to be called. The time when a new and boldly conceived ecclesiasticism, with an apostolic and reversionary type of orders, was to emerge from the somewhat complicated conditions and relations of the Methodisms of the Old and the New World was now but a matter of weeks. Asbury, who had created the possibilities upon which these

8   (113)

things were predicable, was the pivot upon which their enactment was to turn.

Immediately after the treaty of peace, which gave independence to the American Colonies, Mr. Wesley was able to read the necessity for a new and democratic ecclesiasticism befitting the spirit of the young republic. But in this, as in all his enterprises, he moved slowly, and took but one step at a time. He had long had a desire to visit America in person, but the seven years of war had put that thought beyond him. He was now advanced in years much beyond fourscore, and must needs commit to another the offices in which he would fain himself have served his children beyond the Atlantic. Early in 1784 he settled upon Dr. Thomas Coke, a Welshman by birth, a graduate of Oxford, and an ordained clergyman of the Church of England, for this work. Coke was not only the son of a family of high social rank, but he had inherited an ample fortune. Possessed of a naturally ambitious spirit, he entered politics on leaving the university, but soon took orders and was settled as curate in a middle English parish. He expected to rise to distinction in the Establishment, and would no doubt have done so, but was convicted of sin under his own preaching, and on seeking the aid of a Methodist class leader found easement of his burden, and began to preach with evangelical fervor and directness. He was at once accused of being a Methodist, and was shortly afterwards dismissed from his curacy. With but little delay, he visited Mr. Wesley, whom he had not before seen. His gifts, learning, and deep religious experience at once commended him to the now aged leader of Methodism, who had long been looking about for a successor to be

trained to leadership under his own eye. At one time
he thought to lay this responsibility on Fletcher, his
saintly associate; but Fletcher could never be brought
to consent to the arrangement. At a glance Wesley
saw in Coke the man divinely provided. He was under thirty years of age, bore the seal of the Spirit, and
had been, like himself, thrust out to learn the will of
God in persecutions and afflictions. He therefore at
once invited Coke to meet the preachers in Conference,
and from that day to the end of Wesley's life no man
was so much in his counsels as the gifted Welshman.

The subject of the mission to America was broached
to Coke as early as February, 1784. It was then that
Wesley first expounded to him his long-settled belief
that as a presbyter he had, according to usage in the
primitive Church, the same right to ordain that he had
to administer the sacraments, and explained that in
view of his failure to secure relief from the Bishops
of the Establishment he felt justified in exercising his
scriptural right to provide ordained ministers for the
societies in America. The simple and unconventional
proposition, therefore, was that Dr. Coke should accept from Wesley's hands ordination to the episcopacy,
and proceed with that authority to America to ordain
a ministry and superintend the societies. The suggestion was at first received by Coke with misgivings. By
April of the same year he had, however, reached a
favorable state of mind, and, while expressing doubts
as to his fitness for the work, submitted himself to
authority.

At the Wesleyan Conference for the year, which met
at Leeds in August, the matter of the mission was concluded, though the question of ordination was left

open. The preachers were not favorable to the idea, but for that Mr. Wesley considered himself solely responsible. Dr. Coke, Richard Whatcoat, and Thomas Vasey were selected for the American work, and began at once to make preparations for their voyage.

After the Conference Mr. Wesley repaired to Bristol, and Dr. Coke set off for London. Some days later he addressed a letter to Mr. Wesley, fully accepting his views with reference to the proposed ordination, and expressing the opinion that his mission could be satisfactorily accomplished under no less authority than that which Mr. Wesley had offered to confer. The result of this letter was that Mr. Wesley wrote to Coke asking his immediate presence in Bristol and directing him to bring with him the Rev. Mr. Creighton, a presbyter of the Church of England, who had often preached in the London chapels and who was in complete accord with Wesley's work and policies.

On the arrival of Dr. Coke and Mr. Creighton in Bristol Wesley reviewed the arguments for the step he was about to take, which arguments he had pondered for more than a score of years, and then with the assistance of the two clergymen ordained Richard Whatcoat and Thomas Vasey presbyters for America. "Being peculiarly attached to every rite of the Church of England," he thereafter, with the assistance of Creighton, ordained Dr. Coke superintendent or bishop for the work in America, and gave him "letters of ordination under his hand and seal."

In this act the Founder of Methodism contradicted the prejudices of a lifetime to follow the straitly marked path of Providence. In the office of consecrator he acted not as the Churchman, but as the efficient agent of a history that had come to the point of its outgoing. He was impelled to an act which, though he had appraised and judged it in advance, he was at little pains to publicly vindicate. That was for all future times to do. He was shut up to do what he did. The reasons in hand and the logic of history were sufficient; the results were to pass to other years and other generations.

It thus happens that the orders and authority of the ministry of Episcopal Methodism rest upon both an apostolic and historic basis. The type is demonstrably apostolic, and the historic identification is both successional and instant in historic necessity. They are, in fact, the recovery and restoration of those simple apostolic methods and functions which were displaced by constrained interpretations of the evangel. The status of Methodist ordinations in the three offices of the ministry is forever settled in the logic of which these statements are a brief setting forth. The hierarchical cavil in opposition has multiplied itself into unprofitable volumes; but the canons of Methodism, settled in history and providence, are beyond repeal, and find a larger vindication every year.

But large as were the reasonings which guided the mind of Wesley in planning for a new ecclesiastical order in America, and wholly as he rested in the certainty of the divine approval, the human center of his confidence was the personality of Francis Asbury. The whole scheme of the organization, so far as any details were anticipated, revolved around that personality; and when the hour of determination came, it was found that the weight and influence of that personality were supreme. This was unquestionably the scale of the Petrine primacy in the apostolic community. It was not hierarchical or ecclesiastical precedency, but the ascendency of personality. Personality is the basis of the priesthood of history.

A writer from whom I have already quoted sketches a picture of Asbury as he stood amongst his brethren at the moment Wesley was shaping to a conclusion his plans for the settlement of the societies in the New World, and only a few months before the arrival of Coke bearing the Magna Charta of American Methodism. This writer says: "Among the pioneers Asbury, by common consent, stood first and chief. There was something in his person, his eye, his mien, and in the music of his voice which interested all who heard him. He possessed much natural wit, and was capable of the severest satire; but grace and good sense so far predominated that he never descended to anything beneath the dignity of a man and a Christian."

This was the figure which to the vision of Wesley loomed large in the foreground of the possibilities of Methodism in America. It was faith in this man that led him to consent to so large an independency for the societies and to so radical a departure for their government.

Dr. Coke, in company with his associates, Whatcoat and Vasey, arrived in New York on November 3, 1784. No official information concerning this mission had been sent to America, and the arrival of the missionaries was, in consequence, unexpected. Mr. Asbury, who, after the Conference held at Baltimore in the previous spring, had ridden through the Valley of Virginia and parts of Pennsylvania, had been in New York as late as September; but his stay had been short, and he was now touring through the ever-fruitful districts of the Peninsula. While in New York he had learned through letters received from England by John Dickins, the preacher in charge, something of the plans of Mr. Wesley, and he had also had an intimation of the coming of Dr. Coke. But the information was too indefinite to more than feed a hope that sometime— possibly soon—the help so long prayed for by the societies would come. He had not even attempted to forecast the character of the relief to be provided.

Immediately on his arrival in New York Dr. Coke disclosed the secret of his commission to Dickins, and that well-taught and enthusiastic reformer advised him to proclaim it at once. But the legate of Wesley could only reply that Mr. Asbury was first to be "most respectfully consulted concerning every part of the plan and its execution." He accordingly, after a very brief delay, set out to seek Mr. Asbury in the South, where, like another Elisha, his hand was upon the plow in the furrowed field. The first stage of the journey ended at Philadelphia, where a short stop was made, and where Dr. Coke was cordially received not only by the members of the society, but also by two resident Episcopal clergymen, Dr. McGaw, who had coöperated with Asbury in Delaware, and Dr. White, who afterwards became the Protestant Episcopal Bishop of Pennsylvania. Pushing on southward, Coke and his two companions came on November 14, ten days after their debarkation at New York, to Barrett's Chapel, a country preaching place where the famous meeting between Coke and Asbury occurred.

Asbury had learned of Dr. Coke's arrival and also of his southern progress, and had set out to meet him.

Barrett's Chapel was a brick structure, and the most pretentious country meetinghouse of the Methodists in America. It was Sunday, and the occasion of a quarterly meeting. "A noble congregation" was present, additional advertising having been done when it was discovered that so distinguished a preacher was to be present. When Asbury reached the chapel, the service was already well advanced, so that he had no opportunity to speak to Dr. Coke until the conclusion of the sermon. The communion was celebrated, and Asbury was greatly surprised to see Whatcoat, whom he supposed to be only a lay preacher, take the cup in the administration. When the service was over, a memorable scene occurred, which is effectively described in Coke's own words: "After the sermon a plain, robust man came up to me in the pulpit, and kissed me. I thought it could be no other than Mr. Asbury, and in this I was not deceived." An eyewitness says that the other preachers were melted by the scene "into sweet sympathy and tears," and that the whole assembly, as if struck "with a shock of heavenly electricity, burst into a flood of tears."

Coke and Asbury were entertained together at the Barrett home, not above a mile from the chapel, where, as soon as they were in private, Coke opened the nature of his mission. This was simply to ordain Asbury to the episcopacy that they might thereafter ordain the preachers, or so many as might be necessary to supply the ordinances to the societies, and that the whole work might have a scriptural basis and a scripturally constituted superintendency. Neither Wesley nor Coke had provided beyond this for the organization of a Church, showing how much had been trusted to the judgment and initiative of Asbury. He met the exigency without hesitation. Indeed, although he had but an imperfect understanding of Coke's instructions, he had already provided for a council of preachers to receive and pass upon the matters submitted. When Dr. Coke opened to him the plan of a joint superintendency and the ordinations, he was at first shocked, the departure being so radically contradictory of his preconceived High-church notions. He determined at the outset to do nothing without the consent and votes of the preachers; and most of all was he determined not to accept the general superintendency without election by the whole body of his fellow-itinerants.

A council was accordingly called, and the letter* of

---

*The text of this famous letter follows—viz:

"BRISTOL, September 10, 1784.

"*To Dr. Coke, Mr. Asbury, and Our Brethren in North America.*

"By a very uncommon train of providences many of the provinces of North America are totally disjoined from the mother country and erected into independent States. The English government has no authority over them, either civil or ecclesiastical, any more than over the States of Holland. A civil authority is exercised over them, partly by the Congress, partly by the provincial assemblies. But no one either exercises or claims any ecclesiastical authority at all. In this peculiar situation some thousands of the inhabitants of these States desire my advice, and in compliance with their desire I have drawn up a little sketch.

"Lord King's account of the primitive Church convinced me many years ago that bishops and presbyters are the same order, and consequently have the same right to ordain. For many years I have been importuned from time to time to exercise this right by ordaining part of our traveling preachers. But I have still refused not only for peace's sake, but

Mr. Wesley and the statement of his legate were laid before it. The decision was that a *general* Conference should be called to convene in Baltimore at Christmas-tide. Freeborn Garrettson was commissioned to summon the hosts for the moot. Riding north and south, he spread the call so widely that long before the time appointed every itinerant in America, with possibly a single exception, had heard. That exception was Jesse Lee, who was laboring in the far South.

In the meantime Asbury planned extensive preaching itineraries for himself and Dr. Coke during the six weeks that remained before the Conference should sit. Fitting Dr. Coke out with a horse, he added "Black Harry," his own servant, a negro lay preacher, who, though ignorant of letters, was famous for native

---

because I was determined as little as possible to violate the established order of the national Church, to which I belonged.

"But the case is widely different between England and North America. Here are bishops who have a legal jurisdiction. In America there are none, neither any parish ministers; so that for some hundreds of miles together there is none either to baptize or administer the Lord's Supper. Here, therefore, my scruples are at an end, and I conceive myself at full liberty, as I violate no order and invade no man's right, by appointing and sending laborers into the harvest.

"I have accordingly appointed Dr. Coke and Mr. Francis Asbury to be joint superintendents over our brethren in North America, as also Richard Whatcoat and Thomas Vasey to act as elders among them by baptizing and administering the Lord's Supper. And I have prepared a liturgy, little differing from that of the Church of England (I think the best constituted national Church in the world), which I advise all the traveling preachers to use on the Lord's day in all the congregations, reading the litany only on Wednesdays and Fridays and praying extempore on all other days. I also ad-

eloquence and a correct knowledge of the way of salvation. In this manner the first Protestant bishop of the New World traveled over a large part of his diocese, preaching, baptizing, and administering the sacrament of the Holy Communion to the people so long deprived of the ordinances. He was received everywhere with enthusiasm and hospitality. The homes of the great people were opened to him, and multitudes thronged to hear his fervent and powerful sermons. He himself estimates that on this tour he baptized more people than he would likely have baptized in a curacy in England during a lifetime. For his own part Asbury claimed during much of the tour planned for himself the companionship of Whatcoat and Vasey. As he journeyed his mind was engaged with the busi-

---

vise the elders to administer the Supper of the Lord on every Lord's day.

"If any one will point out a more rational and scriptural way of feeding and guiding these poor sheep in the wilderness, I will gladly embrace it. At present I cannot see any better method than that I have taken.

"It has indeed been proposed to desire the English bishops to ordain part of our preachers for America. But to this I object: 1. I desired the Bishop of London to ordain one, but could not prevail. 2. If they consented, we know the slowness of their proceedings; but the matter admits of no delay. 3. If they would ordain them now, they would expect to govern them. And how grievously would this entangle us! 4. As our American brethren are now totally disentangled, both from the State and the English hierarchy, we dare not entangle them again either with the one or the other. They are now at full liberty simply to follow the Scriptures and the primitive Church. And we judge it best that they should stand fast in that liberty wherewith God has so strangely made them free. JOHN WESLEY."

ness so soon to come up in the Conference. The
preachers he found everywhere were pleased with the
plan proposed. Why should they not be pleased? Was
it not the very course from which a majority of them
had been estopped in 1780? The time also came when
Asbury himself could say: "I am led to think it is of
the Lord." But he was "not tickled with the honor
to be gained;" he feared there might be "danger in the
way."

During the month of December the lines of the two
itineraries crossed several times, and the General Superintendent and his prospective associate had more
than one interview touching their concerns. The most
important of these junctions occurred at Abingdon,
in the State of Maryland, where it was decided the
first Methodist college in America should be built.
Dr. Coke was driven thither in the coach of Mr. Richard Dallam, a planter, who was in sympathy with the
Methodists. Asbury had already broached the idea of
such an institution, and the land for the same had
been secured. It was now definitely agreed that it was
to be called Cokesbury College in honor of the two
superintendents, and to raise money for its erection
and endowment was to be amongst their first official
undertakings.

At each successive meeting of Coke and Asbury the
reserved and self-taught pioneer grew upon the college-
bred Churchman and ecclesiastical diplomat. In his
journal Coke wrote: "I exceedingly reverence Mr. Asbury; he has so much wisdom and consideration, so
much meekness and love; and under all this, though
hardly to be perceived, so much command and authority."

On December 17 Coke and Asbury met at "Perry Hall," that ever serene retreat, and completed their plans for the Conference. Dr. Coke speaks of the "noble room" provided for him and of his week's stay in that hospitable mansion. Whatcoat joined them on the 19th, and the next day they began the revision of the "Rules and Minutes"—that is, the adaptation of the "Large Minutes" of the English Conference to the needs of the soon-to-be-organized American Church. With such recensions of the Wesleyan categories Asbury was already familiar; so the three made satisfactory progress.

The Conference began its sittings in Lovely Lane Chapel, Baltimore, on December 24, at ten o'clock in the morning. Dr. Coke took the chair, and directed the opening services, which were simple and impressive. It is believed that about sixty of the more than ninety American preachers were present. Some were prevented from attending by the floods and snows, while others received the notice too late to cover the distances that separated them from the meeting place. Several lists of the personnel of the Conference have been compiled, but none is believed to be complete. The detailed official records of the session are not extant, but the order of procedure has been established from the printed minutes and the book of Discipline of 1785, and from other sources.

On Friday, the 24th, was read the official letter of Mr. Wesley. This letter, which has already been referred to as the Magna Charta of American Methodism, reviewed in order the rise of the American republic, the consequent dissolution of the Church establishment in the former Colonies, and the fact that

Wesley had been appealed to by the Methodists in the new republic for advice and help. It then cited the authority which had convinced Wesley of his right to ordain, following upon which was announced the appointment of Dr. Coke and Mr. Asbury to be joint superintendents, and Mr. Whatcoat and Mr. Vasey to act as elders in connection with the work in America. Concluding with a friendly challenge and a brief summary, the letter commits the societies "simply to follow the Scriptures and the primitive Church."

After the reading of this letter discussion of the title and organization of the new Church was begun, and "without agitation" these matters were brought to a satisfactory issue at the afternoon session. As Mr. Wesley had expressed his preference for an "episcopally governed Church," it was decided to call the new organization the Methodist Episcopal Church, "making the episcopal office elective and the elected superintendent or bishop amenable to the body of ministers and preachers."

On Saturday, the 25th, a vote was taken on the question of the election of Dr. Coke and Mr. Asbury to the superintendency. The vote being affirmative, Mr. Asbury was on the same day ordained by Dr. Coke to the diaconate, the function being attended with preaching and an appropriate ritual. On Sunday, the 26th, he was made an elder by the imposition of the same hands, and on Monday he was formally consecrated a bishop or general superintendent. These offices were simple and unostentatious, but as historic events they have acquired an extraordinary significance. In the episcopal consecration of Asbury Dr. Coke was assisted by his two presbyter associates,

Richard Whatcoat and Thomas Vasey, and also by the Rev. William Philip Otterbein, Asbury's close and faithful friend.

Three days, Tuesday, Wednesday, and Thursday, were mainly taken up with the work of passing upon revisions of the English Minutes and the framing therefrom of a Discipline for the use of the new Church. These actions included the adoption of the revised Prayer Book, or "Sunday Service," as it was called, which Wesley had prepared and printed for the use of the American societies. In addition to the abridged Anglican liturgy and else this book contained the original Twenty-Four Wesleyan Articles of Religion, an abridgment of the Thirty-Nine Articles of the Anglican Confession. The Conference added an article, "Of the Rulers of the United States of America,"* which is XXIII. of our Confession, thus making the number twenty-five; hence "the Twenty-Five Articles."

This work ended, the Conference proceeded to the election of a number of the preachers to serve in the offices of deacon and elder. Dr. Coke testifies that these elections were conducted with great impartiality, without show of self-seeking on the part of the preachers, all of whom were young men and men who had barely reached middle life. Asbury's journal says that twelve elders were elected, but the number appears to have been even larger. The title of "presiding elder" did not

---

*This Article was subsequently amended, and a vote is being taken this year (1909) in the Southern Conferences for a further amendment, so as to adapt it to use in lands where the Church has mission fields.

then come into use; but these elders were, it was understood, to be located with reference to groups of societies or circuits so as to give the sacraments to the people and complete the plan for a general oversight of the work. The presiding eldership is thus integrant in the polity of episcopal Methodism. It is an essential part of the episcopacy, which is not so much an office as an idea. The episcopacy does not inhere in a personal incumbent, but in an episcopal body consisting of the general superintendents, or bishops, and the district superintendents, or presiding elders. The office of presiding elder had its genesis in the ordination by Mr. Wesley of Whatcoat and Vasey to serve with Coke in America. They were not called *presiding* elders, neither was Coke styled *a bishop*. At that time Mr. Wesley had but a general notion as to the shape the government of the Church in America would take. It is certain that the episcopacy took a somewhat different shape from that which he contemplated; but the norm of our episcopacy is his consecration of Thomas Coke. Likewise was there a definite officiality implied in the setting apart of Whatcoat and Vasey to the eldership. Their investiture was the complement of Mr. Wesley's idea of a general superintendency.

The American Conference emphasized the officiality of the superintendency by *electing* both Coke and Asbury by a majority vote. At the same time the Conference elected certain men to the eldership with the understanding that they were not only to administer the ordinances, but were to be superintendents of districts or groups of circuits. It is true that the official duties of the "superintendent elders" were few and simple, but so were also the official duties of the bishops. The responsibilities of both offices increased rapidly and in a direction that was not clearly foreseen at the beginning. This was that logical and providential development which marks the fitness of the complementing offices.

The Conference had thus in the space of a single week rounded the outlines of and set upon its historic way the most extraordinary and effective Church organization of modern times. On Friday a number of deacons were ordained, and on Saturday, January 1, 1785, the question of the college at Abingdon was considered, voted upon favorably, and a subscription was taken for the same. On Sunday, January 2, twelve preachers, previously ordained deacons, were ordained to the eldership, and on Monday, January 3, "the Conference ended in great peace and unanimity."

9

CHAPTER XI.

Pledging History.

It was now General Superintendent Asbury. But the simplicity of the man of unworldly ideals and purposes was unaffected by the new dignity. If there was a rising of pride or self-gratulation, it was quickly repressed. A characteristic introspection came with the quiet which succeeded the haste and labors of the Conference. Concerning the feelings revealed by that inquisition he wrote: "My mind was unsettled, and I was but low in my own testimony." Five days later he made this entry in his journal: "I am sometimes afraid of being led to think something more of myself in my new station than formerly." The preventive against an assertion of self was to dedicate himself to be more than ever the servant of his brethren.

But to one impulse born of his new relation he gave the freest rein—a hunger for wider conquests and a more rapid spread of the gospel. What had been before but a hope became now a plan for immediate realization. Even before the close of the Christmas Conference he had cast his eyes southward and southwestward to the very limits of the continent, and outlined his first episcopal tour on a scale commensurate with his expanded vision. He had already, three years before, penetrated North Carolina and planted stations in the fertile valleys of its great rivers, and even beyond the crests of its intersecting mountains. Now he determined to ride beyond the farthest Methodist outposts and come to those parts in South Carolina and

(130)

Georgia that had known, nearly fifty years before, the labors of "the Oxford Methodists." Charleston and even Savannah were objectives in the plan of this first episcopal circuit.

The Christmas Conference adjourned at noon January 3, and on the evening of that day Asbury preached the first sermon after his ordination. The next day he took the saddle. Dr. Coke was to go immediately to New York to superintend the printing of the official Minutes of the Conference and the new Form of Discipline—the first of those unique and potent little volumes that have had so large a place in the reverence of millions of Americans.

The initial stage of Asbury's journey carried him into central Virginia, where he performed his first episcopal office, the ordination to the diaconate of Rev. Henry Willis. Willis had been in charge of the work in the Holston Valley. He had been elected to the eldership by the Christmas Conference, but was unable to reach the place of meeting. From this point Asbury drafted him to be his traveling companion, and ten days later, at a church near the North Carolina line, ordained him a presbyter.

Services were held by the General Superintendent almost daily, and at these the ordinances were administered. Hundreds of infants and adults were baptized, and the people long without the communion were made glad to receive the bread and wine at the hands of their own chief minister. Asbury at this time wore in the administrations and when discoursing the gown and bands of a presbyter of the Church of England, and used the abridged Prayer Book. This conformity was grateful to "the old Church folks"—that is, the former Anglicans, who then constituted the great body of American Methodists. The catholic-spirited Presbyterians also welcomed the Methodist overseer, and, being largely destitute of pastoral attention, gladly received the ordinances at his hands. With the immersionists it was different; they demurred. In a spirit of conciliation, Asbury began to *plunge* such candidates for baptism as preferred that mode; but before the end of the year the practice was discontinued.

On February 10 Asbury and his chaplain (so we may describe Willis) reached Salisbury, where the indomitable Jesse Lee was in charge. The gowns and bands displeased him greatly, and he satirized the innovation so mercilessly that Asbury abandoned it, and, it is claimed, never again appeared in public arrayed in any character of canonical frippery. Only a little while, in fact, did the Prayer Book foible obtain. Neither it nor the surplice was suited to the homely and impromptu spirit of American Methodism. Ritualism is a historic sign of spiritual decadence, and Methodism had then the dew of its youth.

From Salisbury Lee accompanied the General Superintendent and his traveling companion into South Carolina. Passing through the Cheraws, they reached the sea at Georgetown, from which point they passed along the coast toward Charleston, where they arrived on February 24. Somewhat more than two weeks were spent in the Southern metropolis, whose people Asbury found to be proud and religiously indifferent. Nevertheless, the gospel which he and his two helpers proclaimed made "a gracious impression" upon some, especially upon the family of Mr. Wells, a prosperous merchant of the place, whose guests they were during their stay. The seeds were sown; a society was organized later, and placed under the charge of Elder Willis, and Charleston became from that day one of the important posts of Methodism.

From Charleston the northward course returned through Georgetown, where a station was also established, and where Woolam Hickson, "a man of brilliant genius and fine enthusiasm," was put in charge. This remarkable man died a year or two later of consumption. Wilmington was visited on March 19, and on April 20 Asbury and Lee reached Green Hill's, on Tar River, in North Carolina. Green Hill was a wealthy planter, a slaveholder, and a local Methodist preacher. His position was an anomalous one in view of the Methodist rule in force at that time; but he was a man of God, and wrought and hoped for the perfect coming of the kingdom. In after years he migrated to the Cumberland Valley and helped to plant and support Methodism in that Eden of Middle Tennessee. At the Conference held in the spring of 1784 one of the three sittings appointed for 1785 was designated to meet at his house. The date in the Minutes is April 29; but the session occurred nine days earlier. This was to accommodate Dr. Coke, who was present and presided; while Asbury stationed the preachers, which he uniformly did, Dr. Coke deferring to his superior knowledge of the men and the field.

This Conference, which has the distinction of being the first Conference of the Methodist Episcopal Church after its organization, was held, according to appointment, in Rev. Green Hill's house, which was spacious and comfortable. The entire membership of the Conference, including the two General Superintendents and about twenty preachers from North Carolina and Virginia, were entertained under the same hospitable roof. The results of Asbury's tour are seen in the appointments made at this Conference, such circuits as New River, Camden, Georgetown, Charleston, and Georgia appearing in the list for the first time. Beverly Allen was the man to whom "all Georgia" was given for a field. Alas that one who for a time was permitted to hold in the hollow of his hand the spiritual possibilities of a commonwealth should have ended his career so meanly! But thus was history pledged in those beginning days. Thus in that then remote Southwest was started the cause which through a century and a quarter has grown mightily in the records of the kingdom.

Ten days later the two General Superintendents attended together the Conference sitting in Virginia. The question of slavery was uppermost with the Methodists at this time, the occasion being a petition which the Conference was to send to the Virginia State Assembly, asking for the immediate or gradual emancipation of the slaves. It was agreed at the Virginia session that Coke and Asbury should visit General Washington and solicit his aid in presenting this document. On May 26 they were courteously received and dined at Mount Vernon. Washington readily gave them his opinion on slavery, which was deprecatory; but he declined to sign the petition. This appears to have been the end of the scheme, and at the Baltimore Conference, which occurred one week later, the minute on slavery was temporarily suspended. The temperate judgment of Washington on this question, expressed at a crucial hour, proved to be of immense advantage to Methodism. Profiting by his views, which were practically those of the Methodists of the South so long as slavery continued to be an institution, the Church entered upon an era of soberer legislation than had been in contemplation, and thus was left unhampered in its ministry to both master and slave.

With the opening of the Baltimore Conference Asbury completed his first official round as General Superintendent. For the distance traveled, the labors accomplished, and the variety of offices performed, it was by far the most considerable and important single round he had ever made. But, as his after experiences proved, it was but the beginning of miracles in this line. With the close of the Conference, Dr. Coke took leave of the brethren in America, and sailed for England to meet the criticisms of both Methodists and Churchmen when he arrived. The people in and out of the Establishment who at this time understood the merits of Wesley's plan for the settlement of American Methodism could have been counted upon the fingers of the Founder's two hands. But Coke saw enough with his own eyes while in America to give him a confidence that no amount of misjudgment could shake.

Asbury was again alone in the headship of the Church. He also had upon his hands most of the problems which he had before Coke's coming, and not a few new ones. Among the latter none was more difficult than that of the projected college at Cokesbury. A century and a quarter has shown that the building and endowing of a denominational college is an undertaking for men of the will and endurance of giants. Before Coke's coming Asbury had planned a school like Kingswood, in England; but Coke wanted a college. The faith and intellectual responsiveness of Asbury embraced at once the idea of his collegian associate, not dreaming of the unrewarded toils and baffled hopes for which it was to stand in his life.

In June following the session of the Christmas Conference the foundations of the college building were laid, and Asbury preached at the commemoration. This sermon, delivered in the hot and open summer air, completed a collapse upon the verge of which he had been trembling for some time. The invalidism which followed forced upon him a season of rest, which he spent partly at "Perry Hall" and partly at the American Bath, the famous warm springs of Virginia. Being in a good degree recovered by midsummer, he was again active, but for the remainder of the year confined himself mainly to journeys in the Peninsula and contiguous parts.

The order and arrangement of the lately published Form of Discipline became about this time a matter of criticism. On account of its lack of heads and divisions the usefulness of the volume was greatly lessened. This defect Asbury set himself to remedy, and out of his work has grown that order of sections, paragraphs, and indices that make the present-day Discipline an open book to the most inexperienced undergraduate in the ministry.

The first Conference for 1786 was to be held at Salisbury, in February, and the journey thither was begun soon after New Year's. The advance was in a course crudely conforming to a great half circle, with Charleston on the outer plane of the arc. To detail the experiences of that long horseback ride across three commonwealths and back in midwinter would be to repeat details already made familiar in this narrative. But commonplace as they were, they played their part in a great apostolic plan. The sermons, private appeals, oversight, and spyings-out of vantages for future stations were like golden wheat grains cast in amongst the snow crystals and ice shards of a winter field to wake and fruit in after days. It was by such ploddings and toilings as these that the empire of Methodism was built up.

In Asbury's journal of this year mention is made of a "Book Concern." This infant enterprise was under the care of John Dickins, an Etonian, of whose capabilities and attainments mention has already been made. This norm of vast and varied publishing interests today was at first simply a depository in one room of the preacher's house in Philadelphia for the few books, Disciplines, hymn books, Wesleyan standards, tracts, etc., which were in demand amongst the Methodists. But even at this time Asbury mentions that a collection was taken under that head.

Another principal idea of Methodist propagandism began also to take root about this time. On April 30, 1786, Asbury called for a public collection to provide funds for "sending missionaries to the Western settlements." In the simple means employed for handling and directing this collection is seen the remote parentage of the many missionary societies of American Methodism, receiving and disbursing in the twentieth century millions of dollars yearly for the evangelization of the world.

Asbury was now greatly cheered with the outlook of the Church. Not only the day of its liberation, but the day of its entering into heritage seemed to have come. With one accord the people hailed the new order. Church-building became general, the revival was spreading, and churchly enterprises of many sorts were taking shape. The new Discipline was working as though it had had a century of testing. The Methodist spirit was winning along with the spirit of the new nation. Prophecy occluded in the labors of the homely band of Methodist itinerants. They published their message daily "in the face of the sun."

The Baltimore session—the determinative and law-making council—opened on May 8 at Abingdon. It had been hoped to sit in the college; but alas! the walls were now "only fit for covering," and a debt of more than four thousand dollars had already accumulated. That was an incubus indeed. "And money is scarce!" sighed the weary Asbury as he remembered his toils past and his toils yet to come. It was enough to discomfit the most intrepid. As for Asbury, his training did not answer to the task, and for it he had no zest. He was a preacher, a kingdom builder, and not a money raiser or a college agent. Yet in these things he also laid a foundation.

Sixty circuits were listed this year against forty-six at the time of the Christmas Conference. In the appointments for the year appears for the first time the romantic name, "Kentucky." This was one of those "Western Settlements" for which the first regularly collected missionary money of the Church was appropriated. In the year of the Christmas Conference fifteen thousand members, with ninety-three preachers, had been reported; while at the Conferences of this year (1786) the returns had credited to the connection more than twenty thousand members and one hundred and seventeen pastors.

The most noteworthy experience of Asbury during the remaining months of this year was a ride across the Alleghanies to a point on the Ohio River, where he went to satisfy himself of the prospects in that then most western west of America. As he went out he overrode the western-moving emigrant groups, and as he returned he met their ox-drawn caravans, and now he realized as never before the necessity for mobilizing his forces toward the frontier. He read a new meaning out of his own early motto: "A circulation of the preachers." But from this loud calling west he returned only to be mocked by a return, at frequent intervals, of his old maladies. Often they mastered him, and for whole fortnights together he was laid up; but he rallied from each attack, and completed his convalescence in labors and travels through heat and cold, through drought and rain and snow.

At Christmastide he was in Baltimore settling the yearly affairs of the "Book Concern," and struggling with that horse-leech problem, the Cokesbury College debt. Thousands had been spent upon the building, and still not a hall or a chamber was tenantable. But great duties lighten their own burdens through variety. With the new year he was off for another extended Southern tour, Charleston, as before, being the objective. While passing through Virginia he was entertained by "a famous heroine of Christ," Mrs. Ball, who was a kinswoman of Mary, the mother of Washington. She had espoused the faith as preached by the Methodists, and continued to the end of her life a faithful exponent of the doctrines of the Church. The name of Ball is still an honored one in the Methodism of the Old Dominion.

After a journey during which, as Bishop Hurst says, he showed "an infinite disregard of fatigue," Asbury came on March 15, 1787, to Charleston, where he met Dr. Coke, who had but lately arrived from England. From Charleston the two General Superintendents proceeded together to Salisbury, where the first Conference of the year was held some days later. The Minutes of 1786 had fixed the date for May 17; but it was changed by Dr. Coke while yet in Europe to suit his traveling convenience, as were also the dates of the Conferences in Virginia and in Maryland, and thereby hangs a whole chapter of American Methodist history, further reference to which will be made as this narrative proceeds.

Dr. Coke had not wholly pleased the Americans during the five months of his first official visit; but they had not failed to see his good points, and indorsed him as an unselfish man and a zealous servant of the Master. They also greatly respected his ability and learning, and were justly proud of his championship. His aristocratic manners were atoned for by his cordial indorsement of the American republic and his expressed admiration of its leaders; but what the preachers secretly objected to was his betrayal of a sense of authority. They accepted the episcopacy with the understanding that the incumbent of the office was to be the servant of his brethren, *the first among equals.* But Coke's ideal of the episcopacy was Anglican. Moreover, he understood that the government of the Church was to remain in the hands of Mr. Wesley in much the same way as that of the connection in England. As the representative of Mr. Wesley, he therefore felt that in America his power was that of a patriarch. This was not the view of either the preachers or Francis Asbury. From the beginning Asbury had questioned the wisdom of agreeing to obey a man three thousand miles away.

The review at the Baltimore Conference—the determinative session—of the arbitrary action of Coke in changing the dates of the annual sittings brought this whole matter to an issue. The contest was sharp, and for a time "the little Doctor" attempted to justify his course. "You must consider yourselves my equals," he retorted sharply upon Nelson Reed, one of his aggressive critics in the Conference lists. "Yes, sir," was the spirited reply, "we do; and we are not only the equals of Dr. Coke, but of Dr. Coke's King." There was too great a fire of Americanism burning in the bones of the "lesser clergy" for him to hold out. To satisfy his displeased and outspoken brethren he submitted a written pledge that he would exercise no function of his office while absent in Europe or elsewhere, and that he would lay claim to no authority when in America except to preside over the Conferences, ordain, and travel and preach in the connection. A record of this transaction appears in the Minutes of this year.

But a much more important matter than this, though one related to it, was this year determined by the joint action of the Virginia and Baltimore sessions. Mr. Wesley had instructed Dr. Coke to call a General Conference to meet at Baltimore May 1, 1787, and had requested the election of Richard Whatcoat to the joint superintendency with Asbury, and Freeborn Garrettson for superintendent in Nova Scotia. At the

Christmas Conference the preachers had by a unanimous vote bound themselves "during the lifetime of the Rev. Mr. Wesley to obey his commands in matters belonging to Church government." Here was an embarrassing record. Some of the preachers, seeing that they were not present when the agreement was entered into, refused to be bound by it. The general interpretation was that the agreement referred to the forms of polity and administration, and not to those details of election and legislation which come properly under these forms. The utmost that the agreement was thought to signify was the union of world-wide Methodism under Mr. Wesley during his lifetime. It was now plain that the action had been a mistake. The time had come to undo it.

The result was that no General Conference was held. The nominations of Mr. Wesley were not considered, and furthermore, by formal action, the rule of submission to Mr. Wesley was stricken from the Discipline. The revised and rearranged Book of Discipline upon which General Superintendent Asbury and Book Steward John Dickins had been at work since 1785 was published immediately after the Conference of 1787, and conforms to the several actions above described. Thus it was that the autonomy and independency of American Methodism were asserted, and its constitution prophesied within two and one-half years after the adjournment of the Christmas Conference. The powers of the episcopacy had been defined and settled, and the rights of the preachers reserved.

It was also by action of the Conference of this year that the official title, *General Superintendent*, was rendered into its equivalent as used in the English Scriptures, and General Superintendent Asbury became *Bishop* Asbury. As for his associate in office, the honorary title of *Doctor* was then so rare a dignity that the Methodists in both hemispheres declined to know him otherwise than as Doctor Coke.

The five bishops of the Church between Coke and Soule lived and died without honorary degrees, and almost without exception the men of their generation also wore unembellished names. How different the case to-day! Titles which in the times of the fathers stood for exceptional attainments in scholarship and learning have now come to be so promiscuously and even recklessly conferred that they are no longer a certain guarantee of even respectable literary equipment.

CHAPTER XII.

Wrestling with Great Problems.

On New Year's Day, 1788, Bishop Asbury surveyed an Episcopal see as great in area as the continent of Europe outside of Russia. It stretched from Nova Scotia on the northeast to the limits of Georgia on the south, and westward in all directions as far as the overseer might ride or an itinerant might range. Asbury was alone in the administration of this vast charge, his colleague having returned to Europe some time after the Conference of 1787.

The tour which Asbury now planned for himself was to be twice the length of that of any former year, and was to occupy a period of more than nine months. A map of the completed journey resembles somewhat the outlines of a mighty hourglass with its extreme points at New York and the forks of the Broad River in Georgia. Six Conference sittings had been appointed for the year—namely, South Carolina, Georgia, Holston, Virginia, Uniontown (Pa.), and Baltimore. Besides these, however, two additional sessions were called by episcopal prerogative, one in Philadelphia and one in New York. The first Conference was held in Charleston on March 12, and the last at New York near the first of October.

As the Bishop left Virginia, in midwinter, upon the first stage of his tour, the whole State was ablaze with revival—"up to that time the most remarkable awakening in America under the preaching of the Methodist itinerants." Refreshed and fired from contact with

(144)

the testifying multitudes to whom he preached as he passed, he went forth to sound the call on the new and ever-changing frontier. His course was over paths that he knew through the Carolinas; then he crossed the broad Savannah, and entered into regions both strange and wild. There he rallied the vanguard, and sent them forth to spy out the land and set stakes in the virgin soil.

Leaving in Georgia the handful of pioneer preachers and exhorters who constituted the first Georgia Conference, with his companion and a pack horse, he started across the Blue Ridge and its companion ranges for the romantic lands of the Holston, a region to which his thoughts had often turned. The undertaking was by far the most formidable he had yet faced, but the confidence with which he entered upon it had a vaster stay than that which supported the boast of Napoleon when he said: "There shall be no Alps." Encountering first the main axis of the Appalachians, he named it the Mountain of Steel. Striking later the escarpments of the Unakas and Great Smokies, he named them the Mountains of Stone and Iron. But once arrived in the historic valley, he found in the home of General Russell, a famous pioneer and soldier, a rest which caused him to forget his toils. There he met the preachers, and was blessed with a forevision of what was soon to be in those ultramontane lands.

But of mountain passing he had but begun to have a taste. From the Holston sitting of the Conference he turned his face eastward, and crossed the Balsam range into North Carolina. After holding the Virginia Conference, at Petersburg, he turned again northwestward, and crossed the Alleghanies into the far-off Valley of

10

the Ohio, to which he had sent missionaries as early
as 1781. There was now in that isolated field a sufficient work to justify the calling of a Conference, and
this he did, presiding at the sitting while on this journey.

For the year 1789 fully a dozen Conferences had
been appointed. There was a complaint that this number was unnecessarily large, and that the sittings were
too close together, some being not above thirty miles
apart. But this objection could not be urged against
those appointed for Georgia and South Carolina. On
his way to the Georgia Conference Asbury was again
joined by Dr. Coke, who had landed, as in 1787, at
Charleston. The two Bishops traveled together from
March until June, visiting all the Conferences and closing their round in New York. At this Conference a
memorable action was taken. In the year 1788 the
Federal Constitution had been promulgated, following
which General Washington was elected to the Presidency of the republic. On April 30, 1789, just one month
before the Conference sitting in New York, the President elect had taken the oath of office. Bishop Asbury,
whose admiration for Washington was great, suggested that the Conference present to him a congratulatory
address. The suggestion was cordially received, and
the two Bishops were appointed to write the address.
This they did, and the same day it was adopted, and
the Bishops were commissioned to deliver it in person.
General Washington, having been acquainted of the
action of the Conference by Rev. Thomas Morrell, the
local pastor, who had himself been an officer in the
Revolutionary War, prepared a written response of
similar length, and, at a time appointed, received the

Bishops and exchanged addresses with them. The function was a simple but most impressive one.

Immediately after the close of the Conference Dr. Coke sailed again for Europe. It was understood that Mr. Wesley's great age and growing feebleness made it necessary for him to have his chief lieutenant constantly near him. Coke probably had other reasons for recrossing the Atlantic. His concerns were indeed so many and so world-wide, with the Wesleyan missions and with the connections in America and Great Britain, that he has been not inaptly styled "the Foreign Minister of Methodism."

It was during the early part of this year that Bishop Asbury received the famous letter from Wesley—the last communication he ever had from those venerable hands—in which the patriarch of Methodism, then in his eighty-sixth year, accused Asbury of seeking to make himself great. This letter had come of the refusal of the Conference to elect Whatcoat to the episcopacy on Wesley's nomination, and of the rescinding of the rule of submission to Wesley's authority. Wesley had mistakenly held Asbury responsible for these actions. But from the charge he has been fully exonerated by his contemporaries. The fallacy of the arguments against the validity of Asbury's episcopacy which High-churchmen have grounded on this letter has been so often exposed that no attention need be given it here.

The Conferences of the year agreed that the name of Mr. Wesley should again be given recognition in the Minutes and the Book of Discipline. This recognition was not a restoration of the rule of submission, but was simply an acknowledgment of Wesley as a bishop emeritus of the American Church. According to Dr. Coke, the action was intended to recognize Mr. Wesley "as the fountain of our episcopal office and the father of the whole work under the divine guidance." In this relation the name of Wesley continued to stand in the American Minutes until he was called to the fellowship of the Church triumphant.

Although the preachers with practical unanimity, and with the expressed sympathy of Asbury, rejected Mr. Wesley's call for a General Conference in 1787, the need of such a Conference was great. Legislation could only be effected by carrying each measure proposed through a series of sittings. These sittings were considered to constitute one Conference. The Baltimore sitting was the "Upper House," so to speak, where legislation was completed, and which had up to and including the year 1787 a distinct power of confirmation. As the Conference sittings multiplied that method of lawmaking became increasingly more difficult, and was every year productive of new chances of disunion. The Baltimore Conference indeed lost its primacy, and legislation got into the sittings haphazard and came out the same way. A General Conference would no doubt have been called in 1787, except for the fear of the preachers that, in the event of the election of another American bishop, Mr. Wesley would recall Asbury to Europe. Now that this danger was past, through the abrogation of Mr. Wesley's patriarchal authority, a majority favored the early convoking of a General Conference, but strangely enough Asbury opposed it.

It is useless to inquire into Asbury's reasons for this opposition. It may or may not have grown out of a feeling that, as he was not a debater, he would be at a disadvantage when great contests arose in a body upon which there was absolutely no constitutional check. It is known that he feared a general moot of the preachers might result in radically altering the established discipline, to which he was greatly attached. He felt the need of an easier concert, but he doubted the wisdom of reaching it at a bound. He had, in fact, another scheme for the government of the Church. A body called "the Council," composed of the bishops and the presiding elders, was to be created and empowered to take over all matters of legislation and the administrative affairs of the Church, under a limited veto left to each of the Conferences. This scheme, although it came ostensibly from the two Bishops, was almost wholly the work of Asbury. It was carried through the Conferences in 1789 and ratified, as the result of a strenuous insistency on the part of Asbury.

The Council had its first meeting at Baltimore December 1, 1789. The members recognized at once a fatal defect in its plan, which required absolute unanimity to carry a measure. Also any rule vetoed by a Conference suspended the rule in that district. The first step, therefore, taken by the Councilors was to propose a material alteration of the restrictions laid upon them by the Conferences. This made it necessary to carry the whole matter through another round of sittings. Being but little in favor with the preachers at first, this arbitrary action of its members provoked a criticism which prophesied for the Council a stormy future. It was indeed doomed to a brief and inglorious existence; but we may note the stages of its decline in their chronological order.

History has placed a bar sinister on the escutcheon

of James O'Kelley, one of the most gifted and aggressive of the early Methodist leaders. He was presiding elder in the Southern District of Virginia, and by virtue of his office was a member of the Council. In position and influence in the Church he was second only to Asbury. At the Council session he took umbrage at the rulings of the Bishop, but he probably harbored an older and more general resentment. In January, 1790, he addressed Asbury a letter in which he brought against him heavy complaints of usurpation and tyranny. This was the opening gun of the famous O'Kelley controversy, which finally resulted in O'Kelley's leaving the Church and establishing an abortive organization known as "the Republican Methodists," or Church of the O'Kelleyites.

A fair picture of what lay before the pioneer Bishop in 1790 may be had by mentally organizing his circuit from these facts: Fourteen Conferences were to be attended, and these were sprinkled over the face of a vast triangle, whose apex reached to the far-away wilderness of Georgia, and whose base extended from New York City to a point in the Kentucky settlements not far from the present city of Lexington. The time of these sittings reached from February 15 to October 4, and the distance around the mighty course was little short of four thousand miles. Five times during that long ride the Bishop crossed the Appalachian Mountains and swam the swollen rivers that poured through their valleys. But the joy of an apostle filled his heart while he carried the burden of caring for all the Churches. Many were the perils he met, and many the strange stories he heard, as he and the faithful Whatcoat, who was his traveling companion much of the year, pressed on in tireless enterprise. They were often on and near the Indian lands, and in Kentucky heard rumors of freshly perpetrated atrocities. The graves of many victims of the red man's rage were shown them. At one stage in their return journey they were escorted by a company of armed frontiersmen, who traveled together for mutual protection.

The heaviest concern of Bishop Asbury this year was for the Council. It was coming in for criticism on every hand. A few of the Conferences gave it scant toleration, but for the most part it was practically reprobated. At some of the sittings the weary Bishop did not have the heart to so much as mention it, and it was now plain to him that its days were numbered.

But if his cherished dream of Church government was disappointed, he found compensation in reflecting upon the progress of the work. The continent flamed with revival. The interest of the former year in Virginia had spread southward, northward, and westward. As the preachers came into the Conferences they brought the glow of it on their souls; when they departed it was with augmented zeal. This was the year in which the Sunday school movement was formally recognized by Conference action. But Wesley had used the Sunday school long before this in his work in England. Asbury was also at this time projecting primary schools in North Carolina, Georgia, and Kentucky. While in Kentucky he raised a subscription of $1,500 for a school in that territory to be known as Bethel. This enterprise became a source of much worry to him at a later day, and he named it "a miniature Cokesbury." Other schools, especially the one in North Carolina and a later enterprise in Pennsylvania, as also one in Virginia, called the Ebenezer Academy, had happier histories. It is worthy of note also that the school which he still later projected in South Carolina survives to-day in that splendid institution known as Wofford College.

The episcopal labors of the year were practically closed with the presidency over a second session of the Council, which was held December 1, and, as before, in Baltimore. Besides considering its own difficult situation, the Council did little except to recommend a loan of five thousand dollars for Cokesbury College. It adjourned to meet again in December, 1792; but it never reassembled. The General Conference of that year displaced it, and inherited all its functions, and many more.

Dr. Coke was scheduled to reach Charleston from Europe by way of the West Indies about the middle of February, 1791. The first Conference of the year was to be held in Charleston, and the two Bishops were then to take the round of the connection together. For this reason the twelve sittings named for the year were to be held at points east of the mountains, and so arranged that the last should fall at midsummer.

Dr. Coke suffered shipwreck off Edisto Light; but arrived in time to attend the Conference, bringing with him William Hammett, an erratic and gifted young Irish preacher, whose sermons so captivated the Methodists of Charleston that they asked, and then demanded, that he be given them as a pastor. This request Asbury flatly declined to consider. A bitter personal controversy arose over the incident. Hammett followed Asbury to Philadelphia, and made a determined effort to secure the Charleston pulpit. Failing in this, he returned to Charleston, divided the congregation, and established an independent Church, to which he ministered until his death a few years later.

Dr. Coke had come to America determined, as has been supposed, to put an end to the Council and call a General Conference. The meeting between him and Asbury was, therefore, not so cordial as had been their former associations; but Asbury showed his sincerity of purpose and his devotion to the Church by surrendering without a contest and agreeing to a General Conference.

The two Bishops had proceeded in their joint superintendency of the Conferences through Georgia and the Carolinas, and were at the second, or Hanover, session in Virginia when they received the melancholy news of the death of Mr. Wesley. Dr. Coke hurried at once to Baltimore, that he might take the first ship to England, and left Bishop Asbury to complete the visitations of the year alone. Being detained in Baltimore over Sabbath, Dr. Coke was asked to preach a sermon in memory of Mr. Wesley. In this discourse he was indiscreet enough to suggest that the Founder's death had been hastened by the action of the American Conference in rescinding the rule of submission. Although the unreasonableness of this supposition was apparent, it had the effect of further chilling the affection of the Americans for the great and gifted man whom they had received half a dozen years before as their ecclesiastical liberator, and whom they had gladly accepted as their first Bishop.

The plan of the Conferences for the year afforded Asbury an opportunity to take up a long-cherished enterprise—namely, a personal survey of New England as a field for Methodism. In the previous year Jesse Lee, burning with desire for the mission, had been made presiding elder of a prospective New England district, and had been given three or four helpers, two of them veterans. With these he had invaded the land of steady habits and Calvinistic theology. A beginning had been made, and the work was to be immediately reenforced.

Asbury made exceptional preparations for his New England journey. The country was old and the highways were good. Instead of the usual horseback advance, he decided to go on wheels, and secured a chaise for his use. In company with Jesse Lee he set out from New York about June 1. A number of the principal cities were visited, including Newport, Providence, Hartford, New Haven, Boston, Lynn, and Salem. In all these he delivered sermons, and in a few instances met with cordial treatment; but, generally speaking, he was accorded scant courtesy by the representatives of other Churches. His rather disparaging estimate of the type of religion he found may have been unconsciously influenced by something besides theological judgment.

Although he saw little that was accomplished by his personal mission, he returned feeling that at an early day Methodism would come into its own, even in the land of "the Presbyterians," as he termed the Calvinistic Congregationalists, whose altars were still supported by appropriations from the State Legislatures. He believed that Arminian Methodism would find tinder amongst the "decrees." The following year his faith was rewarded by tidings of a revival which began under his preachers in Connecticut. The center of this awakening was at Hartford, where that remarkable man, Hope Hull, was in charge. It was during this revival that a lad of thirteen or fourteen years "joined in society" under Hull, and later asked for license as a preacher. This lad was the famous and erratic Lorenzo Dow, whose sermons and meteoric dashes from the Canadas to Mississippi and back were one of the sensations of the early years of the nineteenth century.

The Conferences (eighteen in number) for the round of 1792 began early, the first two being held before Christmas, 1791. These visitations, which the Bishop found it necessary to complete by the end of September, must have represented in the aggregate nearly five thousand miles. In addition to taking in the stations in Georgia, Holston, and Kentucky, he held a Conference in Lynn, and thus a second time compassed nearly the whole of New England. It was to him a year of great stress. At the height of it he made this entry in his journal: "How much I have suffered in this journey is only known to God and myself." As in 1790, he was while on the frontier in the midst of Indian hostilities, and several times barely missed being set upon by the savages. A whole night he paced a sentry's beat, watching for the redskin foe. Again, after a long and weary mountain ride, he was sheltered at a house protected by armed guards. But all conditions, as all places, were alike to him, so he turned in and slept, with no disturbing dreams. In his journal he wrote: "I do not fear. Nature is spent with labor; I would not live always. Hail, happy death: nothing but holiness, perfect love, and then glory for me!" This is the generation of those who overcome by the word of their testimony.

At the end of his five thousand miles of travel the weary itinerant dragged himself through a storm of rain to Baltimore. He had scarcely more than arrived when, as he tells us, "in came Dr. Coke, of whose arrival we had not heard, and whom we embraced with great love." This was the last day of October. The General Conference was to convene the next day in the Light Street Assembly Room, the meeting place of the early General Conferences.

There has been a considerable difference of opinion as to whether or not this should be considered the first General Conference of the Church. Some of the early Church historians have so named it, but the weight of statement is in favor of including the Christmas Conference in the number of General Conferences and placing it at the head of the list. All the Conferences from 1773 to 1778, inclusive, were *general,* but they were not autonomous bodies, only *conversaziones* conducted by Mr. Wesley's personal representatives and the preachers. The Christmas Conference was empowered under its Magna Charta (Mr. Wesley's letter) to act with no limitations except the rule of "the Scriptures and the primitive Church." The Christmas Conference was a General Conference; but it was more. It was, as Dr. Abel Stevens describes it, "an extraordinary convention," called to create a new ecclesiastical jurisdiction. But after separating these extraordinary powers from the general content, there will be found remaining the identical functions—legislative and jurisdictional—of those assemblies that were later known by the canonical name of "General Conference." The General Conference of the Methodist Episcopal Church, South, at the session held at Memphis, Tenn., in 1894, ordered that the reckoning at the head of its journal should include a recognition, parenthetically entered, of the Christmas Conference as the initial sitting in the series of General Conferences. The position thus taken is historically impregnable.

Asbury contemplated the meeting of a General Conference with much concern, because he feared that radical changes in the organization and Discipline of the Church would be attempted. Early events of the session showed how well his fears were grounded.

The attendance at the Conference was large. There were now more than two hundred and seventy preachers in the connection; and as all were eligible to sit, a vast majority of them appeared. Furthermore, it was expected that, in view of the rapid extension of the work, this would be the last assembly of this character that could ever be held, and this spurred many to attend from great distances. Bishop Asbury modestly declined to share the presidency of the session, and withdrew from the Conference room, asking to be "excused from assisting to make laws by which himself was to be governed." He also knew that he was to be assailed; so he said, "Speak your minds freely," and left the Conference to itself, with Dr. Coke presiding.

Those were the times in which precedents were made. On the first day the Conference drafted rules of order. It was also then determined that only by a two-thirds vote could new disciplinary rules be made, or old ones abolished, but that any rule might be altered or amended by a simple majority. At the suggestion of Bishop Asbury, a "Preparatory Committee" was appointed and directed to bring forward proper matters for consideration in Conference. This was the expiring ghost of "the Council." It proved to be a weir of paper before a flood. Within three days after the Conference opened legislation was being lugged in by the ears, and the tribunal of proprieties promptly demised.

It was now that James O'Kelley came forward with his historic resolution directed against Asbury. The subject of this revolutionary document was, that if any preacher considered himself injured by his appointment, he should have liberty to appeal to his Conference; and if the Conference approved his objection, the Bishop should appoint him to another circuit. This contention was espoused by strong men, and some of them close friends of Bishop Asbury, as Hope Hull and Freeborn Garrettson. On the opposite side were men like Jesse Lee, Thomas Morrell, and Nelson Reed. For a time it seemed that the issue was certain to carry, but after a prolonged debate it was decisively defeated. As a result, O'Kelley and several other members of the Conference left their seats and withdrew from the Church. With O'Kelley went a young Virginia preacher whom Asbury had ordained the year before. He was a choice young man and a goodly, and the soul of Asbury yearned after him. Before many weeks the disaffected disciple was won back, and became Asbury's traveling companion and confidant. That was William McKendree, whose apostolic labors rank only second to those of Asbury in the Church of the New World.

The action of the General Conference in rejecting the measure proposed by O'Kelley settled the appointing power of the episcopacy upon a basis which has suffered no change to the present day. Young Mc-

Kendree, who followed for a time the schismatic O'Kelley, became later the champion of the episcopal prerogative, and was recognized as "the Constitutional Expounder of Methodism."

The Discipline came in for material changes and alterations. Its oft-revised categories were now marshaled into three comprehensive chapters. The first chapter concerned the ministry, the second the membership, and the third included the sections on temporal economy, and the doctrinal tracts and Church offices, or ritual. The prophecy of the "Annual Conference" is distinctly read in the empowerment of the Bishops to "unite two or more districts together" to form a Conference or to participate in a sitting. The title "presiding elder" appears this year for the first time in the Discipline, and the duties of that officer come out more clearly than before.

After a two weeks' sitting the General Conference adjourned, having settled in stronger terms the Church polity, and having provided for a general governing body to sit every four years, "to be composed of all the traveling preachers in full connection," as against the eligibility of *all* the traveling preachers in this and the Christmas Conference.

Thus the historic session, which began in storm and confusion, ended in peace and the promise of victory. Problems that had vexed the Church from its foundation had been solved, and greatly needed legislation had been secured. Asbury saw his desires realized by means the employment of which he had contemplated with dread. After a "sifting and shaking" process, he found his position stronger than before. Dr. Coke praised in the highest terms the abilities, moderation, and unselfishness of the American preachers as exhibited in the debates and votes of the Conference.

With these felicitations, "the little Doctor" took leave of his brethren, and again sailed for Europe, leaving the oversight of the continent to his toiling colleague. It is doubtful if Coke ever at any time fully appraised the possibilities of the American work, or saw how great an opportunity for service he was letting slip in giving so little time to the bishopric to which he had been consecrated. Yet in the hearing of his self-given missionary commission he possibly found his providential sphere.

CHAPTER XIII.

IN THE CENTURY'S TWILIGHT.

THE Annual Conference sessions which followed the General Conference of 1792 began almost immediately, the first being scheduled for November 15, at Alexandria, Va. This was the period of experimentation with the yearly Conference, the evolutionary stage in which that body struggled to reach the type of fullness and permanency. Twenty sittings were indicated in the list for the year; but it is certain that a greater number were held, while at least two in the list appear to have been omitted. The extent to which the episcopal visitations were multiplied and extended is suggested by such new and remote points for meetings as Savannah, John's River, Jonesboro, and Nashville.

The Conference in North Carolina was again held at the home of the Rev. Green Hill, and the preachers reported a total of more than nine hundred conversions for the year in that territory. In South Carolina Asbury lodged at "Rembert Hall," the home of Col. James Rembert, a rich planter, and the Gaius of early Methodism in South Carolina. On many succeeding journeys this hospitable roof sheltered the tired Bishop, and the ministries beneath it cheered and refreshed him for his toils. Indeed, it was the experiences which fell to him in homes like those of James Rembert, Harry Dorsey Gough, Judge White, Governor Van Cortlandt, General Russell, Green Hill, the Dallams, and the Warfields that proved the earthly compensation of his homeless wandering life. It was about this time that he imparted this confidence to his journal: "None need desire to be an American bishop on our plan for the ease, honor, or interest that attends the office." And yet when he compared his lot with others, he counted himself amongst the most blessed of men, and declared in borrowed, though none the less triumphant, words:

> "The things eternal I pursue.
>
> . . . .
>
> The things by nature felt and seen,
> Their honors, wealth, and pleasures mean,
>   I neither have nor want."

Although the General Conference had left him in a stronger official position than before, troubles continued to multiply. The O'Kelley schism was taking definite shape. Systematic efforts were being made by the seceders to lead away large bodies of Methodists, and at one stage of the controversy the scheme was nearly successful. Tidings of these movements followed the Bishop on his distant journeys and caused him much concern. But he proved to be powerful in all parts of Methodism, whether present or absent. A constant correspondence issued from under his hand as he rode and preached and sat in Conference. With arguments, with tearful entreaties, with persuasiveness of love, he won the people back in numbers, and thus reduced the schism to the thin edge; yet for all this, the losses of Methodism from this cause were constant for several years, and it was not until 1802 that the discrepancy in membership was fully covered. This was Asbury's deep affliction, and, saint though he was, he had strong words for those who troubled Israel. Sometimes these strong words went beyond even what he himself in soberer moments could adjudge allowable. "I have said more than was for the glory of God concerning those who have left the American connection," he penitently wrote in his journal, "and who have reviled Mr. Wesley, Mr. Fletcher, Dr. Coke, and poor me. O that I could trust the Lord more than I do and leave his cause wholly in his own hands!" At Savannah he saw the ruins of Whitefield's Orphanage, which had been destroyed by fire. The charred and gaping walls were still standing. While yet a young preacher in England he had seen the copperplate counterfeit of the building, famed through two worlds, and the melancholy spectacle upon which he now looked affected him deeply. Within a few years he was to witness a similar picture at Cokesbury.

A significant episcopal act—the first step in the evolutional movement toward a permanent type of yearly Conference—belongs to the record of this year. That was the uniting of the works in South Carolina and Georgia into what was afterwards known as the South Carolina Conference; but at this time there were neither Conference names nor boundaries. Though the last section of the old colonial empire, except New England, to be invaded by the Methodists, South Carolina and Georgia were yet the first integrants of Methodism to be thrown into permanent Conference shape. Savannah was made a station and put in charge of Hope Hull, who had wrought so effectively the year before in New England. Thus nearly threescore years after John Wesley had left the capital of Oglethorpe between suns a Methodist was again there to combat the vanities and follies of this world.

After leaving Savannah and passing up through the

Carolinas, Asbury again accomplished his long and perilous journey across the mountains into the wild new territory of Tennessee and the distant settlements in Kentucky. By the end of summer he had, in returning, crept again over those stony barriers, and had again completed the round of New England, in which little-while-ago unpromising field he was comforted with the reports of many conversions. By the beginning of autumn he was in Philadelphia, now being visited by a scourge of yellow fever. Unhindered and unterrified, he entered the stricken city, prayed, delivered his message, and then went his way to answer other calls.

There is a limit to human endurance, and this Francis Asbury was often forced, though reluctantly, to acknowledge. Diseased and broken, he was compelled during 1794 to give up his accustomed circuit of the republic. He dared not attempt in his enfeebled condition the passage of "the American Alps," as he termed the triple Appalachian ranges; but contented himself chiefly with visitations through those States which had made his circuit before the meeting of the Christmas Conference. The preachers from distant fields met him at halfway points, and he there planned their stations and directed their future movements. An enforced inactivity of many weeks occurred during January and February, and this season was spent in the genial climate of Charleston.

Practical and matter-of-fact though he was, there was yet in the make-up of Asbury an element of the dreamer and idealist. This was that in him which ran to the seer. Colluding with his faith, it enabled him to see results before they were attained; it gave fascination to adventure, and made enticing the enterprise of the impossible. The distant treadings of his unseen itinerants through mountains and valleys remote were a perpetual echo of music in his thoughts. He had also the rare faculty of divining the spirits, and knew the men whose feet would echo thus. In March, 1794, he writes: "I have provided Brothers Gibson and Lurton for the *westward.*" That was Tobias Gibson; and never was word of command laid upon a more intrepid soldier. The word "westward" had for him a soul-entrancing sound. In 1800, with the call of the new century, he rode to the settlements on the Cumberland, there procured a frail boat, which he paddled down the Cumberland, the Ohio, and thence into the Mississippi, in which stream he continued until he came to the Natchez country, where through successive years he labored and laid the foundations of Methodism in that then more than romantic region. Death early called him to his rest. His dust sleeps within hearing of the eternal roll of the tides of the river along whose banks he sowed the enduring seed.

The Conference held this year in New England was a notable one. After preaching in Boston, where he assured himself that Methodists would "yet have a work," in company with Robert R. Roberts, afterwards one of the bishops of the Church, Asbury came to Wilbraham and met the preachers. Not a few of the men famous in the early history of Methodism were in that little gathering. Besides Roberts and Lee were Ostrander, Mudge, Taylor, and Hull. Stevens, the historian, stopped in his narrative to make special mention of these names of men who "led the triumphs of Israel in the land of the East."

Experience had taught Asbury and the brethren much wisdom in the arrangement of the Conferences. At first there was an unnecessary waste of time and a needless multiplication of meetings. But the districts were now so consolidated that for 1795 only seven sittings were appointed, as against twenty, and even more, in some previous years. All the frontier work was united in one body called the "Western District." This made it necessary for the Bishop to make but one point beyond the mountains, where all the preachers, gathered into a single assembly, made not only an effective show, but held a helpful fellowship.

This year the heart of Asbury was deeply saddened by news of the death of Justice White, of Delaware, his benefactor and protector in the times of strife and war. "He was a friend to the poor and oppressed; he had been a professed Churchman, and was united to the Methodist connection about seventeen or eighteen years," was, in part, the simple eulogy passed upon him by his simple-hearted friend and Bishop. It was about this time also that the journal of Asbury noted the death of Richard Henry Lee, a "great politician, who was active in promoting the independence of the United States." It is significant that in the same connection he sighed over the impotency of the measures, political and ecclesiastical, for dealing with the cause of slavery. The men who made the republic had their own notions about slavery, but left the problem, with all its perils, to the men of an after time.

Freeborn Garrettson, the Roland of the itinerancy, had married a woman of wealth, and was settled in a sumptuous home on the Hudson, but was still loyal to his call as a Methodist preacher, and continued so to the end of his life. Descending the country from his episcopal visitations in New England, Asbury was entertained in the Garrettson home, and also tarried a day with his long-time friend, Governor Van Cortlandt, whose manor was in the same quarter. Van Cortlandt was one of the truly great figures of his day. He had won renown in public life, but was heartily religious. He was a tower of strength to the Methodists. In his home Washington, Lafayette, and other distinguished men had been entertained, but they were not made more welcome than were the itinerants. Whitefield had several times been his guest, and from the balconies of his mansion had addressed a multitude of people. The highest compliment which Asbury could pay to this courtly publicist and hearty Methodist layman was that he reminded him of General Russell, the pioneer soldier Christian, now sleeping under the sod of the far-away Holston Valley.

Bishop Coke was expected in the country to preside over the General Conference of 1796. Asbury therefore began in the autumn of the previous year his seventh round of the connection with the feeling that relief from the great burden he was carrying was soon to be afforded by his colleague and his brethren. It seems incredible that he should have been left so long without episcopal assistance, but more incredible that at the next General Conference the episcopacy was not "strengthened;" but why it was not done will be seen when we come to review in their place the proceedings of that body.

It becomes now no longer necessary to follow the apostolic pioneer around his six thousand miles of

circuit. He had come to know the passes of the
"American Alps" and the paths of the wilderness as
seamen know the sea. Each year he pushed his own
advance a little farther westward, and flung the battle line a stage beyond his own going. Each year, too,
a step farther northward, as a step farther southward,
pressed the vanguards which he was all but daily re-
cruiting, and still he declared it impossible to supply
preachers for the work. In the South the itinerants
were in sight of the Spanish possessions, and in the
North they were invading the "Province of Maine"
and pushing up the courses of the Canadian rivers. At
the turn of the year word came from Jesse Lee that
the bulwarks in New England were giving way, and
that even Boston was receiving the Methodists. Asbury
estimated that this year there were seventy thousand
Methodists in America and the West Indies. The Minutes showed a total of nearly three hundred preachers
connected with the work. When, twenty-five years
before, Asbury entered upon his labors in the New
World there were with himself and Richard Wright,
his fellow-missionary, but eight Methodist preachers
on the continent, and scarcely five hundred members
in society.

A memory of his initial days of service in America
was revived to him this year. The episcopal round
closed with the Conference in Philadelphia, and here
Asbury had the pleasure to receive as a visitor at the
Conference his old-time comrade in arms, Joseph Pilmoor, who was now rector of a Protestant Episcopal
parish in the "City of Brotherly Love." The ex-
itinerant was not only cordially received, but was invited to preach, and Asbury expressed gratification at

hearing "such wholesome talk" from his "plain countryman."

And now having learned through the medium of the newspapers that Dr. Coke had reached Baltimore, he rode to "Perry Hall," where he gave himself up to a "rest of both mind and body." Despite their sometime sharp differences, there subsisted between Coke and Asbury a deep and sincere personal affection. Asbury not only admired the great and commanding talents of his colleague, but cherished a profound respect for his faithful and unselfish zeal in the cause of God. For his own part Coke regarded Asbury as being, next to Wesley, the most apostolic man he had ever known. It is certain that Asbury always breathed easier and felt a surer confidence when his colleague was within easy access. In an entry in his journal touching the General Conference which met a few days later he says: "Bishop Coke was cordially received, as my friend and colleague, to be wholly for America, unless a way should be opened to France."

About one hundred preachers reported at the opening of the General Conference. The new rule cut off not a few, and many eligibles were too remote to undertake the long journey. But the giants were there, and the old battle on the episcopal prerogative had to be fought over. Asbury described it as "a stroke at the presiding eldership." There is no record of what this stroke was exactly; but a later time developed it into a matter known and read of all men.

The entire work was now divided, or rather consolidated, into six Annual Conferences, with definite boundaries and distinct names. These Conferences were the New England, Philadelphia, Baltimore, Virginia, South Carolina, and Western. The first, as its name indicated, included all New England. The Philadelphia Conference included all of New York, the eastern third of Pennsylvania, New Jersey, Delaware, and the eastern shore of Maryland; in the Baltimore Conference were found those parts of Pennsylvania and Maryland not included in the Philadelphia Conference. The entire State of Virginia and the northern half of North Carolina were designated as the Virginia Conference, while the remaining half of North Carolina and all of South Carolina and Georgia went to make up the South Carolina Conference. Kentucky and Tennessee were described as the Western Conference.

And now it was that the interpretative jurisprudence of Methodism began. By vote of the General Conference the Bishops were directed to prepare explanatory notes on the various sections, rules, and provisions of the Discipline. This was done, and the "Notes" were printed in the tenth edition, the one bearing date of 1798, and from these "Notes" have grown the official "Manuals" and other expanded commentaries on Methodist law and constitution used in the various branches of the Church to-day.

Bishop Asbury expected and desired the election by the General Conference of one or more "assistant bishops," but he set his ideal so high that the body hesitated to act. Not, indeed, that there were not men in the body who felt that a fit man could be found; but the few who felt that way were unable to concentrate the judgment of the majority. Asbury was then asked to select his own colleague or colleagues. This he steadily declined to do, and the problem was thereby made more difficult of handling than before. It was at this juncture that Dr. Coke came forward with a proposition that seemed to offer an instant and complete solution. His relations in Europe had been strained for some time, and he was doubtful as to what his future course should be. He now agreed to settle in America and give his whole time to assisting Bishop Asbury, except when he should be engaged in looking after the missions in the West Indies or France. The preachers were much divided as to the wisdom of adopting this course; in fact, as we have seen, there was much opposition to Dr. Coke, and his apparent neglect of the Americans had not helped to remove this feeling. But as he was already a Bishop of the Church, and now agreed to serve under terms satisfactory to his brethren, and as Bishop Asbury strongly urged the adoption of that course, no bishop was elected, and Dr. Coke's proffered services were accepted. This arrangement promised much for Asbury's relief, but it was disappointing almost to the last degree.

The two Bishops proceeded together on the round of the Conferences until February, 1797, when Dr. Coke sailed for Europe to return within a short while, and thereafter, as both he and the brethren expected, take up his permanent residence in the New World. Asbury was at this time suffering acutely from his old maladies, and during this year was in bed oftener and longer than during any previous period. He was confined fully six months out of the twelve, and sorrowfully records that he was able to travel during the year not above three thousand miles. He was also much weighed down with general despondency. The going away of his colleague caused him deep regret. "To-morrow," he says, "my dear Coke sails for Europe. . . . Strangers to the delicacies of Christian friendship know little or nothing of the pain of parting." Beyond any question Dr. Coke was sincere in his desire and purpose to return and become a settled bishop in America, but in Europe he found conditions that he had not supposed existed. He was, in fact, agreeably surprised to discover that his brethren in Ireland and England were demanding his release from the obligation given the Americans, that he might serve the home land. A year before he had believed his welcome in Great Britain to be gone. The happy discovery of this preference confused his feelings and left him in a strait betwixt two.

So it was that the invalid Asbury was left to struggle on through his year of toils, with none to share the heavy demands of his office. On September 23 he made this entry in his journal: "I received a letter from Dr. Coke. As I thought, so it is, he is gone from Ireland to England, and will have work enough when he cometh here. . . . It is a doubt if the Doctor cometh to America until spring, if at all until the General Conference. I am more than ever convinced of the propriety of the attempts I have made to bring forward episcopal men."

One thing is clear from the above, and from other like records—namely, that Asbury did not hesitate to propose a particular man for the episcopacy. Whether or not he was wise in doing so in *his* time it is now impossible to say; but a modern Methodist sentiment has ruled strongly against "nominations" for the episcopal office.

Giving up hope of help from his colleague, Asbury turned, as before, to his solitary task. He attempted to meet the preachers in the Western Conference, and even crossed the mountains, but was forced to return, leaving the administration to the presiding elders. More than once he was forced to call an elder to hold the Conferences in Virginia and other States. Jesse Lee was his trusted substitute, and at this time he strongly favored Lee for the episcopacy; but when, in 1800, Lee failed of election he and his friends were inclined to charge his defeat upon Asbury. The story is one of painful human misunderstandings.

To Asbury's surprise, no doubt, Dr. Coke did return to the continent in the autumn of 1797. On November 15 he presided at the session of the Virginia Conference, and to that body presented an official letter from the Conference in England asking for his release from the obligation to reside in America. This it was not the province of a yearly Conference to grant; but the preachers gave their personal consent to an abrogation of the agreement. Dr. Coke remained on the continent until the following spring, preaching and doing the work of a bishop. He then sailed for Europe, and returned not until the General Conference of 1800.

The year 1798 had a cheerless opening for Asbury. He was still extremely feeble, and felt that his end was nigh. Weak in body, nervous, and unable to read or study, he employed himself in winding spool cotton and talking to the children and slaves of the home in which he was a guest. His mind was abroad in the vast new lands where the scattered Churches needed his fostering oversight; but heaven had decreed to him months of inactivity, and these he spent in fireside ministry to the little ones. Sublime adaptation! At times he was able to do stints of work, and such times he put on his journal, preparing it for publication. The book business of the Church had greatly prospered; but alas! the faithful Book Steward, John Dickins, who to Asbury was as another soul, this year fell a victim to the yellow fever, and was gathered to his rest. This and news from England of the death of his aged father added heaviness to the continued bodily afflictions from which he suffered.

As the year advanced his strength increased, and he was again able to take up his visitations; but he determined to give himself to the simple work of attending the Conference sessions. The last Conference of the year was held in New England, where fifty preachers assembled, such had been the growth of the work in the short space of seven years. It was at this Conference that Lorenzo Dow was received on trial as a traveling preacher and began his extraordinary career. With the close of this Conference Asbury turned slowly toward the South, and entered upon a short midwinter stay in Charleston, which he had come to regard with an affection and interest only second to that which he cherished for Baltimore.

The episcopal work for the next year (1799) was curtailed somewhat. Six Conferences only were appointed, and these were scheduled to sit between January and July. A note appearing in the Minutes of 1798 and 1799 reads: "Jesse Lee travels with Bishop Asbury." In previous years the Bishop had seldom traveled without a companion. Henry Willis had ridden with him in 1785, on his first episcopal tour; Mc-

Kendree had accompanied him in 1792; while in 1790 Whatcoat had with him crossed the mountains into the new territory, and had shared his hardship and all but tragic adventures. Lee and Roberts and Hull had gone with him about New England, and no journey had ever been made to the Southwest without companionship; but the Conference appointment of a regular chaplain spoke the extreme point to which his strength had wasted. Lee took the burden of his work, the preaching, the presiding, when the Bishop was not equal to the demand. In a word, the plan was to ease him of everything except the stationing of the preachers and the ordinations. More than once Lee went forward and held the Conferences, Asbury having drafted the stations and anticipated as best he could from his sick room the difficulties of administration.

A somberer touch was soon to be added to his already depressed feelings, for in the last days of the old century Washington had died, and the news was slowly drifting toward him in his far southern retreat. His admiration for Washington had been boundless. Two men—one in the temporal, the other in the spiritual realm—had seemed to him ideal. These were Washington and Wesley. "I am disposed to lose sight of all but Washington, matchless man!" he wrote. This was the once loyal subject of King George, whose conscience would not permit him to take a provincial oath of conformity. But this also was the man whose conscience, whose faith were compelled to respond at last to the demands of right and truth. This was indeed the element of absolute greatness in Asbury—he submitted to be led, to follow truth whether manifested in subjective convictions or in arguments read from the force and facts of life about him. He was seer and hero in one.

And now it was that a thought which had shaped itself in his mind a year before deepened into a purpose. This was that at the coming session of the General Conference he would surrender the episcopal office into the hands of younger and stronger men. He had even selected, and set his heart upon, the two men who were to take up his work. And thus it was that he saw the century of Wesley and Washington fade out.

CHAPTER XIV.

Answering the New Age.

From the New Year's session of the Conference at Charleston to the new century session of the General Conference was but a step. After the Charleston sitting had concluded its labors, Asbury dispatched his chaplain, Jesse Lee, on a visit to a number of the more western outposts to see that the itinerants were in their places, while he continued his rest in Charleston, if such a laborious lay-off as he was there taking could be called rest. Lee having returned from his mission early in February, the two set out on their return northward, with Baltimore as a destination.

The General Conference opened in Baltimore and in the canonical first week in May. Bishop Asbury describes this Conference as one that indulged in much "talk" and yet did "little work." There was little that needed to be done, and surely it was a great comfort to him that the body kept its hands practically off the Discipline. The Church is perhaps happiest when the general body finds least to do. Certainly it is a salutary rule to avoid unnecessary legislation.

But several important matters engaged the attention of the Conference. Two full days were given to a consideration of the double relations of Dr. Coke to Methodism. It will be remembered that a letter from the English Conference had been brought by him to the brethren in America in 1797, requesting that he be released from his promise to reside amongst them, since there was the most urgent need of his services

12 (177)

in both England and Ireland. This letter had at first been read to the Virginia Conference; and while that body had no power to act upon it, consent was given so far as its rights were involved, and the whole matter was left to the General Conference. Asbury had written an official letter to the English brethren explaining the situation, and so the request was now to be acted upon. The Conference, not without reluctance and regret (for Coke had come to be better understood and more highly esteemed), consented "to lend him for a time" to the English brethren, with the understanding that he was to return and take up his residence in America so soon as his business would allow. It was also expressly stipulated that he should return for the General Conference of 1804.

The next action of the Conference was to solicit from Bishop Asbury an expression of his wishes as to the General Superintendency. For some time previous to the meeting of the body the Bishop had seriously considered if he should not offer his resignation. This information he gave out freely to the preachers. He even went to the extent of writing his resignation, with a view to submitting it at the first session of the General Conference; but it seems that the opposition to that course was so great that he reconsidered it. He then submitted to know if the Conference would be satisfied with such partial service as his shattered and enfeebled health would permit him to give. In answer to this inquiry, the Conference by unanimous vote expressed its gratitude and great obligations to him for the many and great services he had rendered the connection, and entreated him to continue in the General Superintendency as far as his strength would permit. Both Asbury and the Conference regarded this action as a practical superannuation. The man whom the brethren saw before them, though but five and fifty years of age, was broken, emaciated, and apparently near the grave. But the bow of the mighty man was only temporarily unstrung. He had yet before him more than fifteen years of apostolic labors. He was yet to catch the step of the new age and lead the hosts to victories now barely dreamed of or wholly unimagined.

The mind of Bishop Asbury being thus ascertained, the Conference by a decisive majority voted to elect one additional bishop. This being settled, the question came up as to what should be his relation to the two original bishops. Should he be an assistant of Asbury, or should he be his equal? This afforded an opportunity for a renewal of the old fight to restrict the appointing power of the bishops; but after many amendments were offered and defeated, it was voted that the bishop to be elected should have equal authority with Asbury.

Following this action the Conference proceeded to the election, as ordered. The expectation of Asbury was that Jesse Lee would be selected by an almost unanimous vote, and that appeared to be the most general forecast; but when the vote was counted a tie was announced, Jesse Lee and Richard Whatcoat receiving each fifty-seven votes. A second ballot was thereupon ordered, and the result was the election of Richard Whatcoat by a majority of four votes. The selection of Whatcoat has generally been regarded as a mistake, and plainly, the circumstances being considered, it is hard to be accounted for. He was ten years older than Asbury, nearly as feeble, of an ascetic temperament, and proverbially impractical. He was, however, a blameless, holy man, and an enticing and effective preacher. But instead of being wings or even crutches to Asbury, he was, in the blunt language of one of Asbury's biographers, "a burden." As a sort of official chaplain to his colleague, he visited the yearly Conferences, presiding and preaching as there was necessity; while Asbury planned the stations and administered affairs in general. After only six years of service the gentle-spirited man was called into rest.

Reference has already been made to the fact that Lee and his friends held Bishop Asbury responsible for his defeat. It has generally been reported that when the tie vote was announced Asbury was desired to say which of the two he preferred, and this he properly declined to do. It is probably upon no more serious ground than this that Asbury was credited with the election of the one and the defeat of the other. I have in my possession while these pages are being written an autograph letter from Lee to Asbury in which their differences are discussed. It is a very humanlike epistle, such as good men have been too often betrayed into writing. It has passed through the hands of at least two great historians of Methodism, who after nearly a hundred years treated it as *private;* I shall not presume to do otherwise.

It is worthy of note that at this General Conference the salary of the preachers was raised from sixty-four to eighty dollars per annum—that was some recognition, in a financial way, of the dawn of the nineteenth century. Bishop Asbury is to be credited with a measure adopted at this session requiring the yearly Conference to keep permanent journals of their proceedings and send them to the General Conference for inspection. By this means the connectional administration of Methodism has been assured, and a world of historic material created and preserved.

Asbury at last had a colleague upon whose presence he could count. They were already bosom friends and intimate traveling companions; so there was no time required to get acquainted and agree upon an itinerary. Three of the scheduled Conferences for the year remained to be held. The first of these was in Delaware, and thither the two Bishops, accompanied by Jesse Lee and others, repaired. The Conference was a Pentecost. Bishop Asbury estimates that one hundred conversions occurred during the sitting. This was only a repetition of what had happened at the General Conference a fortnight before. In fact, the revival which had swept Virginia, Maryland, and the other Southern Conferences had leaped across the Chesapeake and caught in Delaware and the Jerseys, and was moving northward every day. When the two Bishops came to hold the Conference in New York late in June, the spirit of awakening was found to be equally manifest in that quarter. Bishop Asbury wrote: "We have had a mighty stir in the Bowery Church for two nights past until after midnight; perhaps twenty souls have found the Lord."

With the customary end-of-summer, or autumn, round through New England and down the "pleasant banks of the Hudson" Asbury was back in Maryland and at "Perry Hall." But he met a sad situation in that once homelike place. "The walls, the rooms no longer vocal," he wrote; "all appear to be hung in sackcloth. I see not the pleasant countenances nor hear the cheerful voices of Mr. and Mrs. Gough. She is in ill health, and writes: 'I have left home perhaps never to return.' " With a heavy heart he turned from the portals of his former happy retreat, and looked far away toward the wilderness and the mountains where he was soon to be.

And now all but a miracle had happened: the afflicted, broken man who stood before the late General Conference ready to resign his office was restored to health, or rather to what passed with his thankful heart for that blessing. In company with his colleague and William McKendree, who had been for several years presiding elder on the Western Virginia District, he set his face toward the most western stations of the Church in Kentucky and Tennessee. As they went out they heard the very winds that outdrove them ringing with hosannas, for the revival had gathered volume every day since the General Conference, and one thousand conversions had been reported in the Virginia and Baltimore Conferences. They were to hear in the far wilderness a like sound, for the fire had been borne thither in zealous hearts and was burning fervently. In fact, the great mid-continent revival which marked the opening of the nineteenth century had already begun.

McKendree was in the vigor and promise of his wonderful manhood, and was going out himself to take charge of a vast diocese in the West. As presiding elder of the "Kentucky District" he was to have oversight of the Methodist stations in the States of Ohio, Kentucky, and Tennessee. Later, his authority was to extend from the Scioto in Ohio to the Natchez settlements on the lower Mississippi. Six years and more he wrought in and watched over this imperial heritage, at the end of which time the Church, as by inspiration, called him to the office and work of a bishop.

Over an accustomed route the Bishops and their companion entered Kentucky; but from Bethel, where the Conference was held and where Bishop Asbury wrestled again with his "miniature Cokesbury" problem, they pushed on westward and southward several stages beyond the farthest point previously reached by Asbury. They were now in Middle Tennessee, and their destination was Nashville, the thriving young city on the Cumberland. In his journal Asbury says: "I rode to Nashville, long heard of but not seen by me until now." The first church of the Methodists in that capital was built of stone. It was at this time in an unfinished condition; but Asbury opined that when completed it would be "a grand house." It was, however, used on the occasion of the visit of the three august men, each delivering a discourse within its walls, McKendree having the honor of speaking first. The church, which was afterwards named in his honor, has had several successors, but has maintained a vital witness until this day.

The old-time camp meeting, which exercised so great an influence on Methodist evangelism for three-quarters of a century, originated amongst the Presbyterians and Methodists in the Cumberland Valley about the beginning of the nineteenth century. It was during this journey that Asbury had his first experience with this Christian Feast of Tabernacles. The camp was near Nashville at a place called Dickinson's. The Bishop draws a vivid picture of it: "The stand was in the open air, embosomed in a wood of lofty beech trees. . . . Fires blazing here and there dispelled the darkness, and the shouts of the redeemed captives and the cries of precious souls struggling into life broke the silence of midnight." They heard in the West the echo of the Spirit's work in the East, and, so assured, turned their faces thankfully toward the sunrise. Passing out of Tennessee, the two Bishops entered North Carolina, and, thridding the scenic course of the French Broad River, they crossed the mountains and came again into the salty airs of the Atlantic seaboard.

The second year of the century was distinguished by the recovery of the membership lost to the connection by the O'Kelley schism. This year the numbers in society reached approximately the figures reported in 1791, the year before O'Kelley's departure; but the autumn of 1801 and the spring of the succeeding year totaled a net addition to Methodism of nearly fourteen thousand members, so mighty and so general had the revival been.

This year also brought Asbury a new and effective champion in the controversy with O'Kelley. This astute polemic was Nicholas Snethen, a young and eloquent itinerant whom Asbury chose to be his traveling companion during much of the Conference year. Snethen's answer to O'Kelley proved "an end of controversy," and the O'Kelley ghost was permanently laid. Snethen afterwards achieved much distinction, and was elected chaplain to Congress; but the record had an anomalous end: he at last rejected the idea of the episcopacy which he had defended, and became one of the founders of the Methodist Protestant Church.

Nevertheless, this honest departure has never discounted him in Episcopal Methodist annals. His name is a heritage of the whole Wesleyan house.

It was accounted by Asbury a providence that the sitting of the Virginia Conference brought him into that State about the time of the death of his much revered friend, the Rev. Devereux Jarratt. Although Jarratt had not maintained his former close and cordial relations with the Methodists after the organization of the societies into a Church, his relations with Asbury had never been disturbed. His evangelical spirit had left him in constant isolation from his High-church brethren, and the memories of the old Virginia days of the first revival had been mutually sweet to him and Brother Asbury. The Methodist Bishop preached the funeral of the dead churchman, and left in his journal a tender and grateful tribute to his memory.

In October the episcopal party was in South Carolina. The disturbance of the public mind in that State over the very stringent rule and recommendations on slavery voted by the General Conference of 1800 was great, and Asbury was much perplexed. He himself, while most pronouncedly antislavery, saw the necessity for handling the matter delicately and discreetly, and for the most part his example was followed by the preachers. He came at last to doubt if the legislation of the Church on the subject had been wise, and wished for some wholesome and dependable rule. He did not live to see enacted the very wise legislation of 1816, under which the Church lived in undivided prosperity until 1844.

But the observant Bishop found in South Carolina

at this time a matter more in the way of religion than any controversy on either economics or ethics. Eli Whitney's cotton gin was making cotton the most marketable and the most profitable article produced in all America. This meant not only the perpetuity of slavery for an age, but it meant the rapid accumulation of wealth and the consequent neglect of religion by those engaged in the great and multiplying enterprises thus begotten. In reviewing the outlook the unworldly Bishop remarked: "I cannot record great things upon religion in his quarter, *but cotton sells high.*" The history of the fleecy staple has been a tragedy as well as a triumph.

The names of the Annual Conferences appear for the first time in the Minutes of 1802. The districts had been entered under appropriate names in the records of the previous year. Thus was perfected the method of designating the larger and smaller divisions of the connection which obtains in all the branches of American Methodism to-day. There were seven Conferences in all, and the two Bishops attended these together, beginning with the Kentucky and ending with the New England.

The deepest sorrow of Asbury's life was visited upon him while he was presiding at the Baltimore Conference. The first winds of April—the breath of spring that woke the peach and apple buds along the highlands of the Chesapeake—brought from England a ship with tidings of the death of his mother. After thirty-one years of absence from that "very dear mother," his love for her was as tender and as loyal as when a lad he sat at her knee in their humble Handsworth cottage. A tear-stained page in his homely diary is devoted to her blessed memory. Regularly his itinerant salary was divided with her, and it was this devotion that explained in part the fact that he had himself not dreamed of wife and home.

Later in the year news came to him that his long-time antagonist, O'Kelley, was ill. Asbury promptly dispatched two of his preachers as messengers to the sick man's chamber. The result was that O'Kelley expressed a desire for a visit from his former associate. Asbury promptly responded to the request, and the two so long estranged met in peace and communion. No reference was made to the sundering issues that had long lain between them; but they prayed and parted in love, perhaps, as each one thought, to meet no more on earth, and so it proved. In the original papers of Bishop McKendree I find an autograph letter of a member of the General Conference of 1816 who had had an interview with O'Kelley, and in this letter expressed the belief that O'Kelley and his preachers were ripe for a compact of reconciliation; but if any attempt to accommodate was ever made, it failed.

Bishop Whatcoat's health had now begun to seriously fail, and for part of the next year he was left out of the episcopal itinerary, Bishop Asbury being accompanied into the West at first by Wilson Lee and then by Henry Boehm, a son of Martin Boehm, a coadjutor of Otterbein in the conduct of the German Connection.

At the midyear Conferences Asbury discovered a distressing condition of Church finances. The Baltimore Conference, indeed, was the only one on the continent that appeared to be solvent. At this distance, that which was made a virtue of by the early Methodists—namely, the cheapness of the cost at which they maintained a ministry—is seen to be the weak point of their system. In the midst of ever-multiplying plenty the liberality and large-spiritedness of the Church were repressed by a mistaken standard of asceticism set for the ministry. It retarded the institutional growth of the connection, and made the incipient causes of missions, education, and Church extension unnecessarily difficult. It also restricted whatever growth was realized in these directions to an ideal both imperfect and disparaging. It was one of the struggles of Methodism to break over these precedents and clothe itself with the progressive spirit of the new age. An early symptom of this rennaissance was the gift about this time of three hundred pounds by Miss De Peyster "for the bishops and clergy of the Methodist Church." A similar gift had been noted by Asbury some years before.

The New England Conference for 1803 was held in Boston. A Methodist chapel had been completed and furnished, and the Conference sat within sight of the dome of the proud new Statehouse which Asbury pronounced "one of the most simply elegant buildings in the United States." This session of the Conference in the land of the Puritans was distinguished by the ordination to the eldership of Joshua Soule, a man of whom Methodism was destined to hear, and to the power of whose personality it was to respond in history-making and history-marking crises.

The New York Conference met at historic and picturesque Ashgrove, on the upper Hudson. To Ashgrove Philip Embury, the Haecks, and other loyal Methodists of New York had emigrated at the breaking out of the Revolutionary War, this territory being then within the British lines. Here Embury had gathered a society, and here, dying as the result of an accident, he was buried, and here his grave may still be seen. The place is now within the limits of the city of Albany; but the name has been given to the Church whose history preserves the traditions of the "Palatines."

As Asbury turned from the Conferences in the East to take up his journey to the frontier West, he rejoiced in spirit over the ingatherings of the year. It shows how careful and exact he was in all things that he should in his offhand "computations" have missed the official figures afterwards compiled by only a trifling difference. "By a fair and accurate computation," he wrote, "I judge that we have added, exclusive of the dead, the removed, and the expelled and withdrawn, 13,300. Our total for the year 1803 is 104,070 members. In 1771 there were about 300 Methodists in New York, 250 in Philadelphia, and a few in Jersey. I then longed for 100,000; now I want 200,000—nay, thousands upon thousands."

The Cumberland camp meeting idea so impressed Asbury that his advocacy of it brought the preachers in the eastward pioneer territory to adopt it. A great camp was projected on the Monongahela for August, and to this camp Bishop Asbury and his companion rode on their way into Ohio and the Kentucky and Tennessee Districts of the Western Conference. A multitude of four thousand people attended the ministrations of the Sabbath in the wilderness tabernacle. The scene was midway between the pentecostal centers of the East and the West.

In crossing the Ohio River into the great new State

of that name the Bishop and his party had a sight of
the flotilla of Colonel Meriwether Lewis, recently commissioned by President Jefferson to explore the vast
Northwestern regions watered by the Missouri and
Columbia Rivers. In the earlier months of the year
the "Louisiana Purchase" had been completed with the
ministers of Napoleon, and the enterprising President
was making haste to fix and claim, against the encroach-
ments of Great Britain, the far Northwestern boundaries. Thus silently and without exchange of saluta-
tions at the fords of the shrunken river passed the
chiefs bent on empire, the one to extend the dominion
of the spiritual and the other the dominion of the
temporal.

In Ohio the Bishop enjoyed the hospitality and fellowship of Governor Tiffin, the first executive of the
State, and "a distinguished figure in the history of early
Methodism west of the Alleghanies." In Kentucky
he was the guest of a scarcely less distinguished man
and Methodist. This was Dr. Hinde, who had been a
surgeon under General Wolfe, the hero of Quebec.
Before his contact with the Methodists he was an infi-
del. His wife being converted under the preaching
of the itinerants, he blistered her head "to cure her of
her madness." "But, blessed be heaven," he used to
say, "that blister cured me of *my* madness." He
heard the Methodists, was converted, and became a
saint. Perhaps his greatest distinction is that he was
the maternal grandfather of Bishop Hubbard Hinde
Kavanaugh, one of the Boanerges of Southern Methodism.

New Year's Day, 1804, found Bishop Coke again
in his sometime see in America. The first yearly Con-

ference was held at Augusta, Ga., with Coke presiding. Asbury made the appointments, amongst them one for Bishop Coke to preach all the way from South Carolina to Boston before the meeting of the General Conference. "I mark this year," he wrote, "as the greatest that has ever yet been known in this land for religion." In passing through Charleston he preached in "the great house" which Hammett had built and which had lately come into the hands of the regular Methodists.

We have already referred to one of Asbury's reasons for choosing a celibate life. In his journal of this year he sets down seventeen others, each one of which might be considered by a woman as sufficient. To his plea in extenuation he adds this observation: "If I have done wrong, I hope God and the sex will forgive me. It is my duty now to bestow the pittance I have to give upon the widows and fatherless girls and poor married men." There is a delicious touch of humor in that last clause. In this connection the note is suggestive that he proceeded immediately to Norfolk and organized a woman's society, on which act he comments as follows: "At a meeting of the women we laid the foundations of a female charitable society similar in plan to those in New York and Baltimore, but more liberal. May this live, grow, and flourish when I am cold and forgotten!" Are not the strongly organized and splendidly efficient women's missionary, parsonage, and aid societies in modern Methodism an answer to this apostolic prayer?

As the General Conference approached, Asbury had his usual introspections, and rigidly reviewed his own motives. In his journal he wrote: "I lived long before

I took upon me the superintendency of the Methodist Church in America, and now I bear it as a heavy load. I hardly bear it, and yet dare not cast it down, for fear God and my brethren should cast me down for such abandonment of duty."

The General Conference met on May 7, 1804, and, as always before, in Baltimore. Only one hundred and seven voting members were present. There was no absorbing issue before the Church. Bishop Coke as Senior Bishop presided, and from the chair read the Discipline section by section, and the Conference reviewed each point and considered if revisal or improvement should be attempted. The Book Concern, which since the death of John Dickins had been under the care of Ezekiel Cooper, was ordered to be removed from Philadelphia to New York. The Twenty-Third Article of the Confession was changed so as to recognize the nationality of the United States. A time limit of two years was imposed upon the pastorate. This was done on a motion that had been preceded by no particular agitation or demand, and which apparently provoked but little discussion on the Conference floor, so inconsequential was the origin of a rule which, with slight modification, held through nearly a hundred years in the largest body of Methodism in America, and still holds in that body which is second in importance on the continent.

Asbury made several motions, it being then admissible for a Bishop to take the floor, the most important of which was that an assistant book steward and editor be elected, which vote was put and carried. The question of slavery was, as usual, taken up, and a motion prevailed that the bishops be authorized to write a chapter which should carry a section acceptable to the North and another acceptable to the South. Asbury declined to undertake such a task. The result was that the former rule was much modified, and the Conferences in the South were exempted from its operations. After agreeing to a continuance of the arrangement for Dr. Coke to retain his residence in Europe, laying again the ghost of the anti-presiding eldership agitation and disposing of sundry impracticable motions and schemes, the General Conference adjourned.

Coke, Asbury, and Whatcoat were never to meet again in General Conference. This was Coke's last visit to the Church in America. Bishop Whatcoat died in 1806, and so from that date Bishop Asbury was again alone in the episcopacy until the election, in 1808, of his masterful and apostolic associate, William McKendree.

13

CHAPTER XV.

ABETTING THE MAKERS OF THE CONSTITUTION.

WITH the beginning of the second quadrennium of the new century Methodism had entered upon the era of the making and settling of a permanent constitution for its government. Although Bishop Asbury was not the originator of the idea of a delegated General Conference, or of the constitution under which it was to enact laws and administer power in the Church, he was in keenest sympathy with the leaders and the ideals they represented. He was also in a position to abet their plans and secure their success in the end. This it is the purpose of the present section of our study to show, as the narrative proceeds in orderly detail.

Four yearly Conferences remained to be held after the General Conference of 1804. Three of these—the Philadelphia, the New York, and the New England—the bishops attended together. From the North they descended by the accustomed route of the Hudson Valley and the Highlands, and finally drew rein at Baltimore, whence they had originally set out, having been somewhat more than two months on the round. Whatcoat was in failing health, while Asbury, having suffered a return of former symptoms and having procured to have himself blistered on the neck and foot, cupped and bled, and drenched with heroic emetics, was—though, strange to say, alive—in a mood to make his will and again meditate resignation from office. The empiricism to which he submitted is at this day unbelievable.

It is to be noted that this year the connection suffered a loss of forty-eight itinerant preachers by reason of their taking the local relation. This was largely due to the parsimonious allowances made for the regular pastors. Several of these retiring brethren went promptly into pulpits of the Protestant Episcopal Church, where better salaries invited them, and where as men of action they were both wanted and welcomed. Thus early did Methodism begin to supply its younger Anglican sister with ministers, a service which she has continued to render to this day. In this irregular way the evangelical spirit has been much aided in that communion. It is to the credit of Bishop Asbury that he treated these departing brethren with much courtesy, and even hospitably sped their going. Of one prominent case he wrote: "I am willing that he should belong to the (Episcopal) Church people. I believe that they have more need of him than the Methodists have." And this in no sinister spirit.

In August the journey into the Western Conference was begun. On the way westward Asbury stopped to visit with his friends, the Goughs, who were sojourning at the Warm Springs. Both the master of "Perry Hall" and his wife were invalids, and it was only a few years after this that the master of the Hall passed away, with his faithful friend and Bishop at his bedside. Asbury knew no more devoted friendship than that with Harry Dorsey Gough.

The two Bishops had proceeded on their western tour as far as the Ohio region of Western Virginia, when Bishop Asbury was prostrated, and further advance became impossible. Whatcoat offered to continue the journey alone; but that was both impracticable and undesirable. On a general proposition, his health was more precarious than that of Asbury's, and Asbury saw that it would be better to leave the holding of the Conference to the "President Elder," William McKendree, whom he already foreknew as a colleague.

There was now nothing left the two invalid Bishops but to drift slowly through the eleven weeks of autumn toward their winter asylum at Charleston, at which point the first Conference for 1805 was to be held. A stop was made at "Rembert Hall," where Asbury tarried a time and meditated upon the death of three of the most efficient preachers of the connection—Wilson Lee, Nicholas Watters, and Tobias Gibson—and where Conference memoirs of the two latter were prepared.

Francis Asbury was now the best-known as well as the best-beloved man in all America. In every city in the republic from Savannah to Boston he counted his personal friends by the scores and hundreds. In every village, on every farm and plantation lying near the great highways, in the remotest western settlements, his name was familiar to merchant and laborer, to master and slave, to woodman and squatter. The newspapers heralded his comings and goings, and people of every rank and station attended upon his ministry.

I have nowhere in the course of this narrative attempted to describe Bishop Asbury's preaching or to appraise his pulpit powers. That could not well be done. His sermons answered to no criteria and his powers were entirely too unique to be described in terms of ordinary criticism. He was not a great preacher. He had neither the attainments nor the gifts to make a great preacher ; and yet there must have been an indescribable skill displayed in his manner of handling a subject. He was simple, direct, evangelical. Above everything, he was in earnest. His voice was musical, his appearance reverend and commanding. It was impossible to separate the sermon from the man. His life coalesced with his gospel, and therein was his power. That it was that made him so mighty amongst men.

It was now near the end of Thomas Jefferson's first term in the Presidency, and the political parties had pretty well defined their issues. Asbury discovered that the Methodists were not disposed to hold together on political matters, but showed an independency of thought and action which he greatly commended. "Our people think for themselves," he observed ; "and are as apt to differ in politics (so do the preachers) and divide at the hustings as those of any other denomination ; and surely they are not seekers of the offices of this world's profit or honor. If they were, what might they not gain in many parts of the United States!" Even then they held a balance of power by reason of their preponderance as a religious body. But what Asbury here observed is still true—namely, that Methodism is so thoroughly a religion of spiritual motives and ideals that it can never be enslaved by a partisan political mastery. There is in it too much of the intellectual and ethereal to admit of its being employed for any human aggrandizement.

The health of both Asbury and Whatcoat was improved by their brief winter rest, and they set off from Charleston to visit the series of Conferences appointed for 1805. At Fayetteville, N. C., an early capital of the State, the Methodists had no house of worship except a plain structure which had been built by Henry Evans, a most remarkable negro local preacher. It was known as the African Church. When Asbury reached this place in his northward journey, he was offered the Statehouse for his service, but he declined. Then the Presbyterian pastor tendered him his church, which was a large and pretentious building, but this he also courteously declined, and went with his congregation to the meaner structure used by his own people, saying: "Home is home; ours is plain, to be sure; but it is our duty to condescend to men of low estate." Asbury was a *Methodist* Bishop. If there were those who questioned his ecclesiastical right to bear the title of *bishop,* there was none who doubted his right to wear the name which qualified his title.

Through episcopal indorsement and recommendations the camp meeting was coming into vogue in the Atlantic Conferences, and Asbury's journal gives account of a whole series of these extraordinary gatherings, attended often by from six to eight thousand people, and at which literally thousands in the aggregate were converted. The battle for spiritual dominion was being waged on every side. In some Conferences the supply of ministers was sadly inadequate; in others a number could be spared, and so the *transfer system* was early developed. It was the period of evangelism extraordinary. Of pastoral work in the proper sense there was—there could be—little, except what was done through the class leaders who were in that and the earlier day really an order of subpastors. The preacher himself was never in one stay. The more ground he covered and the more sermons he preached, the better he met the ideal and the need of his office. Pastoral work under these conditions was all but impossible. Asbury estimated for this period twenty thousand additions to the membership of the Church and twenty thousand deficit on quarterage. He thankfully concluded that it was better to have grace than gold, and went on struggling with the deficits. The age of pastoral teaching and training, as also of systematic giving, was yet to come. The evangelism of the time was intensive to an extraordinary degree, but the mastery of congregations awaited the completion of the campaign of conquest.

In July Asbury received a letter from Dr. Coke announcing his marriage. With this announcement came the intimation that he would like to settle permanently in the superintendency in America, provided the requisite number of Conferences would recall him. The experienced Asbury saw how impossible such a proposition was, and counted Coke as lost to the work on this side the Atlantic. A benedict Methodist Bishop was as useless in America at that day as a king. The Annual Conferences declined to recall him. Later he resubmitted his proposition looking to an equal division of the connection between himself and Asbury; but the General Conference followed a wiser and more Methodistic plan in providing for the superintendency of the Church.

The two American Bishops felt equal this year to the task of riding again the mighty circuit of the West; and this they did, passing, as in 1803, through Ohio and then down into Kentucky and Tennessee, across

the vast diocese, quaking with revival, over which
McKendree was still presiding. Asbury had made a
simple, but to him and the Church a most important,
discovery. It was now possible, if only barely so, to
cross the mountains and traverse even the great western reserves in a wheeled vehicle, since a semblance
of highways was appearing. He accordingly before
leaving the East provided himself with a stout light
road carriage, which he describes as a "Jersey wagon."
Thus equipped he was able to travel and make long
journeys, which had become impossible to him on
horseback. For the remaining ten years of his life
he seldom traveled otherwise than in a sulky or light
barouche, which became as much identified with his
apostolate as had his faithful gray before.

At the turn of the year he complained of failing
eyesight, and admonished himself thus: "I must keep
my eyes for the Bible and the Conferences." Within
a week, or ten days at most, this entry follows: "From
Monday to Saturday, among other occupations, I have
been employed in reading a thousand pages of Mr.
Atmore's Memorial and Mr. Wesley's Journal." It
was in this way that he spared his eyes, as it was in
this way that he spared his whole body.

Bishop Whatcoat started out with his colleague to
attend the Conferences of 1806; but early in April the
summon came to halt. He was then at Dover, in the
State of Delaware, and in the home of noble Richard
Bassett; and here he awaited his translation, which
came on July 5, 1806. In the memoir written by Asbury and read before the Conferences of the ensuing
year appears this Asburian sentiment: "Although
Bishop Whatcoat was not a man of great erudition, yet

probably he had as much learning as some of the apostles and primitive bishops, and doubtless sufficient for the work of the ministry." The memoir closed with this interesting summary:

> "Converted September 3, 1758.
> Sanctified March 28, 1761.
> Began to travel in 1769.
> Elected Superintendent in May, 1800.
> Died in Dover, Delaware, July 5, 1806."

In view of the certain early death of Bishop Whatcoat and the feebleness of Bishop Asbury, a proposition had been put on foot by the New York Conference to call an electoral Conference of seven elders from each of the seven Annual Conferences to meet at Baltimore on July 4, 1807, for the purpose of "electing, organizing, and establishing a permanent superintendency and for other purposes." Bishop Asbury favored the creation of such an electoral college, and four Conferences indorsed the plan; but in the Virginia Conference under the vigorous leadership of Jesse Lee it met complete defeat. In this he wrought a great and monumental service.

Asbury was now completely alone. Whatcoat had been removed by the hand of providence, and the Conferences had plainly intimated to Dr. Coke that they disapproved of his removal to the American continent. The electoral Conference scheme had also been disallowed. The connection had declared its faith in Asbury and in providence. The confidence of the Church was that Brother Asbury would be spared until the General Conference of 1808, when the episcopacy could be legally and regularly strengthened. If no bishop should be living when the Conference met, one could be elected, and the elders could consecrate him just as Wesley had consecrated Coke. The fear of "a break in the succession" disturbed nobody. Methodism had "followed the Scriptures and the primitive Church" in 1784, and could do so with equal confidence in 1808. There was no leaning upon canons or traditions.

The solitary Bishop was equally confident and serene, and went his way as in so many years before. Every Conference on the calendar was met, and he had strength for the arduous labors demanded at each. At the Western Conference, though the reports showed that fourteen hundred members had been added during the year, such was the imperfect financial plan of the work that many of the preachers lacked for even necessities. The "father confessor" journal of the Bishop gives us this secret in an entry made while on the ground: "The brethren were in want, and could not provide clothes for themselves; so I parted with my watch, my coat, and my shirt." No fiction touch of Victor Hugo in describing Monsignor Bienvenue surpasses this touch of reality in the daily life of the first Bishop of American Methodism. In 1805 he gave to the world the grounds of his episcopal claims. They were: (1) Divine authority; (2) seniority in America; (3) the election of the General Conference; (4) ordination by Thomas Coke;* (5) the signs of an apostle

---

*The episcopal parchment of Bishop Asbury read as follows—viz.:

"*Know all men by these presents,* That I, Thomas Coke, Doctor of Civil Law, late of Jesus College, in the University of Oxford, Presbyter of the Church of England, and Superintendent of the Methodist Episcopal Church in America,

that were wrought in him. These signs increased with his years.

At the opening of 1807 he rejoiced in what appeared to be perfectly restored health. His New Year's dinner was eaten under a roof of fragrant pine trees on the route northward from Sparta, Ga., where he had held the "South" Conference some days before. The wide round of the year through the Carolinas, Virginia, the Middle States, and New England was but little varied from the experience of former years, except for a journey through the White Mountains, where he encountered snow in May, and an extended tour through the lake region of Western New York, where Methodism was taking ready root. From this region he descended through Western Pennsylvania, where he visited the two Moravian settlements of Nazareth

---

under the protection of Almighty God and with a single eye to his glory, by the imposition of my hands and prayer (being assisted by two ordained elders) did on the twenty-fifth day of this month, December, set apart Francis Asbury for the office of a deacon in the aforesaid Methodist Episcopal Church. And also the twenty-sixth day of the said month did by the imposition of my hands and prayer (being assisted by the said elders) set apart the said Francis Asbury for the office of elder in the said Methodist Episcopal Church. And on this twenty-seventh day of the said month, being the day of the date hereof, have by the imposition of my hands and prayer (being assisted by the said elders) set apart the said Francis Asbury for the office of a superintendent in the said Methodist Episcopal Church, a man whom I judge to be well qualified for that great work. And I do hereby recommend him to all whom it may concern as a fit person to preside over the flock of Christ. In testimony whereof I have hereunto set my hand and seal this twenty-seventh day of December, in the year of our Lord 1784.   THOMAS COKE."

and Bethlehem. The throngs to which he preached at Conferences, at camp meetings, and in the open fields surpassed in numbers and interest those of all past years. He now estimated that there were more than a hundred and forty thousand Methodists in the United States, and that the Methodist preachers were preaching to two millions of people. The entire population of the republic was then computed to be about five millions. Thus nearly one-half the people of the entire country were under the religious influence of Asbury and his itinerants. Such were the miraculous results of thirty-five years of labor.

The Western journey was this year distinguished by the holding of a Conference at Chillicothe, Ohio, the first Methodist Conference ever held in that State, and the first ever held north or west of the Ohio River. From Chillicothe the Bishop pushed westward for a tour through the Miami country, and then southward across Kentucky and Tennessee toward his eastward destination. As he rode or halted for a brief rest he was engaged in compiling an addition to the Hymn Book prepared for the American Methodists by Wesley in 1784. This was congenial occupation, and at this time the freshness of his youth seemed to have returned. He exulted in spirit and reflected with satisfaction upon a tour that should next year add to his old itinerary the province of Canada and the territory of Mississippi. But this was a dream never to be fully realized.

With a record of daily official cares, passing sorrows, and multiplying joys the story of the tireless Bishop draws itself on through the early months of 1808, and the General Conference was again in session. After twenty-four years of all but undivided responsibility in the episcopacy Asbury was to have a real and in every way a competent associate in office.

The General Conference of 1808 met, as had all its predecessors, in Baltimore. It was composed of one hundred and twenty-nine members. Its leaders were men marked for destiny, and as administrators of the commonwealth they had shone with no less distinction than as the lawgivers of Israel. In the delegations were five men who afterwards became bishops of the Church—namely, William McKendree, Enoch George, Robert R. Roberts, Joshua Soule, and Elijah Hedding.

The time had fully come to settle the Methodism of the New World on a permanent constitutional basis, and the men here assembled were the men destined to do it. The Church had now, in fact, but one Bishop, and he was in sympathy with and wholly committed to the new ideals. Methodism was the most American thing in all America. It typed the restless American soul. Like the star of empire its course was westward, and like the spirit of empire its purpose was conquest. Its motto was not only to keep pace with civilization, but to mark out a path for civilization—aye, to be itself the creator and conservator of civilization. Its ideals and doctrines were a unity. It, therefore, only answered the law of its nature when it sought to preserve that unity and to prevent its ever-expanding forces from being dissipated through lack of regulation. The one answer to its one loud-voiced need was an enduring centripetal compact—a constitution.

The organization of the Church was completed by the writing and adoption of this constitution. The general body being formally convened and having had sundry memorials laid before it, Bishop Asbury called for "the mind of the Conference" on the all-important matter. It was promptly decided that there should be a delegated General Conference and a constitution "to regulate it." Thereupon a committee was ordered, and by the wise foresight of Asbury it was provided to be appointed equally from the yearly Conferences—two from each—fourteen in all. This committee appointed from its members a subcommittee of three—namely, Ezekiel Cooper, Joshua Soule, and Philip Bruce—to draft a report; in other words, to write a constitution, though not even these men realized the full historic significance of what they did. The subcommittee met, and it was agreed that each member should write a separate report. Cooper and Soule made each a draft; but Bruce made no writing. When the two drafts were submitted, Bruce indorsed that made by Soule, and, with slight alterations, it went from the large committee to the General Conference. As then read it differed but slightly from the instrument which has subsisted for more than one hundred years as the Constitution of Episcopal Methodism in its various families.

The advantage which the strong central Conferences enjoyed in the old mass meeting assemblies by reason of their nearness to the sittings and their fuller pastoral ranks was a thing not easily to be given up, and at first there was a determined effort to modify the provisions of the proposed constitution on this point. The sharp difference brought on by this issue at one time threatened a rupture in the body, and the New England delegation asked leave to retire. A number of Western delegates also prepared to leave the sitting. A spirit of concession, however, arrested the disorganization, and the historic document was finally settled in the foundations by a strong majority vote. An effort was made at this time to put a clause into the constitution making the presiding eldership elective; but it failed, and, although many efforts have been made during the past century to alter the rule as then established, it has remained unchanged.

It was no secret that Asbury desired the election of McKendree to the episcopacy, and a sermon which the rustic presiding elder preached before the Conference was so satisfactory in spirit and matter that the delegates concentrated upon him with singular unanimity. Bishop Asbury says in his journal: "The General Conference elected dear Brother McKendree to be assistant bishop." But the old Bishop was greatly mistaken in this. William McKendree was elected an associate bishop, and a bishop he was, every inch of him, and had his apostolate vindicated by signs innumerable.

CHAPTER XVI.

In Apostolic Fellowship.

"The burden is now borne by two pairs of shoulders instead of one; the care is cast upon two hearts and heads," rejoiced Asbury as he went out from the General Conference of 1808. The countenance of his colleague gave him joy and his counsels inspired confidence. The zeal and apostolicity of Asbury were truly matched in McKendree. Moreover, in the rugged and rustic Westerner Asbury was constantly discovering evidences that his coming to power had been an overt providence. In consequence of this discovery he felt the first easement of the burden of responsibility which had rested upon him since the days that Rankin and Shadford left him to the primacy of the societies in North America. The judgment of Coke he had always, with good reason, distrusted; while the incumbency of Whatcoat had only added to his concern and difficulties. Now he saw his own increasing lack of service to the Churches about to be supplied by an associate as wise, as careful, as tireless as himself.

Asbury's feelings at this time are well typed in his journal. Such humanlike matters as sitting for a portrait in crayon and planning for a month's vacation "in the pleasant fields" give variety to his entries. An uncommonly sad entry is also to be noted about this time. Harry Dorsey Gough, his long-loved friend, had died near the opening of the General Conference, and his pall had been followed to the grave by the members of that body. On the fifth of June to a great throng

(208)

standing in the open Asbury preached a sermon in memory of the dead. "The discourse was very much a portraiture of Mr. Gough's religious experience and character," which illustrated both the inconstancy of human flesh and the miracle-working power of divine grace. Gough had known the ecstasy of faith and the bitterness of apostasy; but his days had closed in clear and perfect light. Asbury thus saw the friends and events of his earlier ministry passing into memory and history.

The first official sitting for the new episcopal year was that of the Western Conference, calendared to begin October 1, at Liberty Hill, twelve miles from Nashville, in the State of Tennessee. McKendree had already turned his face westward, and, passing through the territory of his former district, crossed the Mississippi River and entered the Missouri Valley settlements in the lands recently acquired from the French. He was thus the first Methodist Bishop, or as for that the first Protestant Bishop, to cross the great midland waters and establish a diocese in "the ultimate West." Fire fell from his lips as he went, and on his return he left a revival burning through the settlements for a hundred miles up the romantic valley.

About July 1 Asbury began a slow journey westward, with the Conference session to be held in the Cumberland Basin as his objective point. For a traveling companion he had engaged Henry Boehm, a strong-bodied, consecrated itinerant, of whose father, a German minister in fellowship with Otterbein, we have already heard. Asbury's object in selecting Henry Boehm was not only to have a companion in travel, but also through him to reach the people of the numer-

14

ous German settlements in the Ohio Valley. In this office Boehm developed great efficiency, and for several years traveled with the Bishop in his wide circuits. His notes of their many itineraries are full and spirited, and are valuable side lights of the Asburian story.

The course mapped out by Asbury for his journey lay through the States of Maryland, Ohio, parts of the territory of Indiana, and thence through Kentucky and Tennessee to the southernmost dip of the Cumberland Basin. More than once the ailing and feeble Bishop sank under the exhaustion caused by the hardships of travel, but rose again, sometimes on crutches, sometimes half borne in the arms of his companion, to enter a church or mount his horse for another stage. Nor was the journey a profitless one by the way. In chapels, in cabins, and at camp meetings in the wilds scores, perhaps hundreds, of people professed converting grace. "I rejoice to think there will be four or five hundred camp meetings this year. May this outdo all former years in the conversion of precious souls to God!" mused the faithful man as he rode through the straining new lands dotted only here and there with settlements.

The old-time camp meeting has never been fully appraised as a primordial force. It not only gave fervency and carrying power to early religious experience exposed to the unfriendliness of pioneer crudeness and ignorance, but it served to create and cement social affinities that resulted in an instant use of sympathy and coöperation, and which also typed and determined the spirit of the settled community in an after time. To trace the silent influences of the Asburian apostolate on our national life one must fully study both his personal and his official relations to the men and women who lit these watch fires of faith and fellowship across the continent.

Indian summer, with its haze and calm, was clothing the hills of Tennessee when Asbury and his companion entered the Cumberland Basin, where Bishop McKendree met them and conducted them to the seat of the Western Conference. The scene of the sitting was a camp meeting to which the itinerants had gathered "from Holston, Natchez, Opelousas, Missouri, Illinois, Ohio, Kentucky, and Tennessee." In the neighborhood of the camp ground was the new home of the Rev. Green Hill, whose name is indissolubly linked with the early history of Methodism in North Carolina, and in this home the business sessions were held. It was the first Conference which McKendree attended as a bishop. It is to be inferred from the tone of Bishop Asbury's journal that McKendree took only a minor part in the administration of the session. He was naturally in the rôle of training and introduction for a time; but he early laid hold of the helm of affairs with a strong hand and a confident spirit. He saw the necessity for and early adopted an orderly plan for "bringing forward the business of the Conference." Much to the disturbance of Asbury, he began to call the presiding elders together to consult in making the appointments, and thus it is to him that Methodism owes the "cabinet," and the placing of the presiding eldership in possession of its logical and historic function as an integrant of the episcopacy. It is indicative of Asbury's confidence in McKendree's wisdom and foresight that he at last cheerfully acquiesced in every advance which his colleague proposed.

The synod in the wilderness having concluded its business, the two Bishops, with Asbury's companion, Boehm, started across the mountains eastward for the round of the Atlantic Conferences, whose sittings were to run into the middle of the year 1809. The next in order after the Western was the South Carolina, or, as Asbury laconically puts it, the "South" Conference; and this was their present objective, though a great preaching and visiting detour was made through parts of North Carolina, with the inevitable circle through Charleston, which was a stage or two from the seat of the Conference at Milledgeville, Ga. The Senior Bishop's notion was that the people should see and know their General Superintendents. His labor was to show himself the servant of all; and in this purpose and its execution he found his associate no whit behind himself. Together in "a thirty-dollar chaise" they rode their wide circuit, did these two primitive, heroic, apostolic Bishops. On their journey "great news" came to them concerning revivals in every quarter. Baltimore and Bohemia Manor, the early loves of Asbury, had been blessed with extraordinary visitations. "Camp meetings have done this!" exclaimed Asbury, adding a new strophe to his song of tabernacles.

Of course the Asburian rote of reading, writing, prayers, and meditations went on daily. It would seem that as the travels of the sexagenarian Bishop increased his capacity for reading also increased, for his journal tells constantly of incursions into new volumes, though they were generally of the same class as those read in earlier years, and so could not have suggested any strikingly new ideals or brought to him radically fresh interpretations of life, manners, or theology.

The Conference session in Georgia is now chiefly
memorable as the one at which William Capers was
received on trial into the traveling connection.   As
preacher, editor, educator, missionary secretary, and
bishop, the name of William Capers remains one of
the chief glories of our history.   As "the founder of
the missions to the slaves" he will be remembered,
perhaps, when every other claim to renown has been
disallowed.   He early grew into the affection and confidence of Asbury, and the pictures which he sketched
of the tenderness, simplicity, and human kindness of
the venerable Superintendent are pleasing in the extreme.

The Conference in Georgia had been held during the
Christmas-New Year week.   Through the snows and
biting winds of January the two Bishops and their
companion proceeded to Tarboro, N. C., where the
Virginia Conference was to begin its sitting on February 1.   McKendree was here amongst his kith and
kin, and took a large share in the administrations.   This
was even now a Conference great in its personnel.   At
least sixty of the itinerants were reckoned by Asbury
to be "the most pleasing and promising young men."
But, with three exceptions, they were unmarried.
Why?   Because the high taste of the Southerners
would not permit their daughters to wed with men
so poor in worldly goods.   "All the better," declared
Asbury, for a celibate clergy was his preference, if
not his ideal.

The question of African slavery, always uppermost
with Asbury, was again on the Conferences, but as
far out of the way of settlement as before.   In his
journal he asks a question which may well be taken

as expressing the crux of the discussion in those earlier years. "Would not an amelioration in the condition and treatment of the slaves have produced more practical good to the poor African than any attempt at their emancipation?" Happily, the question has now only a reminiscential interest. The recital, however, serves to show the sanity and moderation of the first Bishop of American Methodism.

The sessions of the Baltimore, Philadelphia, and New York Conferences, which followed in succession after the "rising" of the Virginians, were without noteworthy incident. In both New York and Philadelphia, however, Asbury had such tangles and annoyances of administration to deal with as caused him to sensibly recall the days of his early pastorates in those cities. The three Conference sessions and the necessary intervals between them carried the episcopal calendar forward to a date near the end of May. In the meantime not a few refreshing experiences came to Asbury and his two traveling companions, McKendree and Boehm, to whom he affectionately refers as "the young men." Calls were made during the northward journey at Baltimore and Barrett's Chapel, both luminous spots in the memory of the Senior Superintendent. At "Perry Hall" he tarried long enough to view the graves of his departed friends, the Goughs. "The image of my dear departed Harry Gough was very present to me," is a touch in his journal at this place wondrously and humanly illuminating. Great friendships are possible only to great souls. Hearing at this juncture that the son of a former familiar in the township of the Goughs had enlisted and gone to serve with the military in New Orleans, he resolved instantly to send a missionary to that far-away city, and wrote to the presiding elder of the Mississippi District to dispatch a man to the new field. Gregory did not more truly covet the Engles than did this man the new-made Americans in the South, nor did the Pontiff act so promptly as did the miterless head of the youngest Protestant sect.

At Barrett's Chapel Asbury had an incentive to review the four and twenty years that followed his meeting with Coke and the adoption of their wise and Heaven-guided plans for realizing the ideals of "the Scriptures and the primitive Church." Amid the shades of this quietude he was visited by his "dear friends, Governor Basset and his lady," who drove nearly forty miles to meet him. A simple tribute paid to simple worth. This man made his friends a part of himself.

Of another sort is the journal note concerning the "steamboat"—"a great invention." This the two Bishops and their rustic Mark saw in the Hudson soon after Fulton had made it a potent and prophetic fact. "My attention was strongly excited," writes Asbury. No man was better fitted than he to measure in a moment of anticipation the meaning to the New World of this tide-climbing invention. He knew the vast distances that separated the nation's centers of life and wealth. He knew also the courses and had measured with his eye the capable bosoms of America's great rivers. In vision he saw the wonders of a time made possible by the magic of steam.

The New England Conference, held at Monmouth, District of Maine, completed the episcopal round for the year. Methodism had struck its roots deeply and firmly in the soil of the land of "the Presbyterians;" but Asbury saw much that displeased and troubled him—much in the land, much in the conduct of Methodist affairs. Most of all, he deplored his own lack of an intimate knowledge of the field and the men. The standard of responsibility which he set for himself in the oversight of the general work was not lower than that which he set for his preachers in the care of their circuits.

By the customary circuitous route through the lake region of New York and southward through Pennsylvania the two Bishops and their companion were at last at the end of the year's long journey. But it was only to begin again the ceaseless round of the continent. Within a fortnight they were in Ohio, on the way to Cincinnati, where the Western Conference was to meet at the end of September. It is indicative of the courtesy and refinement of Asbury's nature that the hardships which he so often endured and the uncouth manners which he so often met did not sap the strength nor dim the perfection of his ideals. Sleeping often on the bare floors of cabins, constantly covered with dust or bespattered with mud in the way, dining on coarse and ill-prepared food, and not seldom amid squalid and unsanitary surroundings, neither the dignity of manliness nor the gentleness of sainthood ever forsook him. In spirit he quickly recognized a discourtesy, and in his soul reprobated a boorish man, though it is doubtful if he habitually expressed himself on such shortcomings except to his journal. To the keeping of that confidant he committed the record of many brutish manners and even personal slights. In one of these records is recited the fact that while he was preaching in a certain place a presiding elder put his feet upon the chancel. This breach of decorum greatly annoyed the one-time saddler's apprentice, whose religion had helped to make him a prince of good manners.

Particularly delicate were his courtesies to Bishop McKendree, although he had written of him at first as an "assistant;" and although the strength and foresight of McKendree often vetoed the judgment of his senior, there seems, in fact, never to have been a serious jar in their relations. When they were separated, as happened in the early part of the second year's journey, Asbury habitually wrote to his associate in a tone of affectionate tenderness, as also of apostolic counsel.

The session of the Western Conference for 1809 must have been something in the nature of a Pentecost. The fires of revival were burning in every direction; and when the two Bishops met at Cincinnati to station the preachers, they found three thousand worshipers ready to join in the devotions. The reports for the year showed that the increase in this field was two thousand six hundred and sixty-six members over all losses.

Turning from the wilderness echoing with the shouts of victorious Israel and glowing with camp fires, the episcopal party found itself at the end of a month on the North Carolina seaboard. It was the eighth time within nine years that Asbury had scaled "the American Alps," as he constantly named the Appalachian chains. In his day he decreed that there should be no Alps.

As was now a custom with him, Asbury took a little

needed rest near the year's end, in the genial and healthful atmosphere of Charleston. Here at Christmastide the Conference sat. That body arising just before New Year's, he immediately set out with his associate on a tour that ended on February 8 at Petersburg, the seat of the Virginia Conference. The land was now filled with memories for the aged itinerant. Nearly forty years had elapsed since he began to ride the reaches over which this journey carried him. "Here were great times thirty years ago!" he wrote. Saith not the Word, "Your old men shall dream dreams?" But this man was a seer also.

A few weeks after this his course brought him to Deer Creek, in the State of Maryland. If the scenes in Virginia had stirred his memories, how must these earlier surroundings have been peopled with spiritual presences? To add to the memory fructifying scenes, he here met Father Boehm and Henry Watters. The places of earth—high places and low—get their meaning from the footprints of life. This was Asbury's last visit to this region, as also his last sight of these venerable men.

At the Virginia Conference Asbury was called upon to decide whether or not the Bishops had the "right to form the eighth or Genesee Conference." His decision was affirmative, and the new Conference to be "composed of the Susquehannah, Cayuga, Upper and Lower Canada Districts," was scheduled to meet at Lyons, State of New York, July 20, 1810. Having officially visited the Baltimore, Philadelphia, New York, and New England Conferences, the Bishops came in due course and time to the sitting of the new Conference. After seeing the business of the body conducted to its conclusion, Asbury expressed the opinion that its creation had been the most judicious act of the joint episcopacy. But the Annual Conferences were not unanimously of this view. There was much criticism of both Asbury and McKendree in the different sittings, and they were charged with exceeding their prerogative; but the Bishops relied upon an unrescinded order of the General Conference of 1796. The matter finally went to the General Conference of 1812, which declared that "the Genesee Conference is a legally constituted and organized Conference." Whatever the construed rights of the episcopacy in that early day to change Conference boundaries and establish new jurisdictions, they passed to the larger prerogative of the General Conference, which must take the initiative and give authority for such administrative acts.

The long and tedious path across the Alleghany Mountains and down the far-stretching Ohio Valley to the center of the Western Conference is now a familiar one. Over this path Bishop Asbury made his way in a sulky during September and October of 1810. In company with Bishop McKendree, Learner Blackman, James Gwin, and Peter Cartwright, he came on November 1 to a chapel in Shelby County, Kentucky, where the Conference was held. The sitting over, the feeble Bishop rejoiced in a reported increase of four thousand members for the year, sold his sulky, and prepared for a winter horseback ride across the mountains into the Carolinas. Unable now to preach with the frequency and force of former years, he adopted a new method of evangelizing by the way. To travelers and at the doors of cabins and farmhouses he distributed small religious tracts in German or English, as his discerning ear or eye dictated. It was thus that he became the pioneer in the circulation of religious tracts and books, a rule that became an effective instrumentality in the hands of a generation or two of Methodist preachers coming later.

It was during this year that Asbury read the history of American Methodism brought out by Jesse Lee. The differences between Asbury and Lee were an open secret, and the Bishop, judging from an entry in his journal, was both gratified and surprised to find that the historian had dealt more considerately with him than he expected. He felt moved to correct but a single statement of the volume, and one which involved a matter of small moment.

At the opening of the new year cheery news came from the North to the two Bishops in Charleston. The troubles in the Genesee Conference which appear to have taken on a connectional aspect were reported composed, and the General Superintendents breathed more freely.

Two noteworthy records were made by Asbury in connection with the Conference round of this year. The South Carolina Conference convened at Columbia, and was held in the parlors of the spacious home of United States Senator Taylor, who, with his family, was in warm sympathy with the Methodists. The members of the Conference were entertained in the many chambers of the hospitable establishment. The Virginia Conferences being appointed to meet in Raleigh, N. C., the State officers hospitably put the Senate Chamber and Hall of Representatives at the disposal of the body. The business sessions were held in the Chamber, while the Hall was devoted to preaching services three times each day. Many converts were claimed, amongst them Secretary of State Hill and several members of his family. The Church was thus greatly strengthened in that center.

In his progress northward the Bishop and his company were entertained at Germantown, Pa., by Dr. Rush, a signer of the Declaration of Independence and a man of renown in his day. At the end of the visit Asbury, who had been professionally advised by the Doctor and his associate, asked what he should pay. "Nothing, only an interest in your prayers," was the reply, both physicians being devout Christians. "As I do not like to be in debt," replied Asbury, "we will pray now," and with that he called the company to prayer on the spot.

At the height of summer, and between the sittings of the New England and the Genesee Conferences, Asbury crossed the St. Lawrence and made a tour of a fortnight's length through Southern Canada. He saw comparatively little of the country, but got a fair idea of conditions there. He saw difficulties, but was cheered with prospects. His patriotic American feelings were deeply stirred while crossing the line. Returning from the hardship of the adventure, he fell, sick and fainting, in the arms of Bishop McKendree, for whom his affection increased each day.

The Annual Conference sessions of the summer, autumn, winter, and early spring returned delegates to the General Conference to be held in New York May 1, 1812. This was to be the first delegated session of that body, and much interest centered around the elections. The absorbing issue then before the con-

nection was the status of the presiding eldership.
Should it remain an office to be filled by the appointment of the bishops, or should the Annual Conferences elect the incumbents by ballot? Asbury was
deeply concerned that the old rule should not be sub-
stituted, and it is certain that McKendree shared his
sentiments. The issue influenced the elections to no
small extent; but we shall see how a conclusion favorable to the old order was reached in the general Methodist mind even before the death of Asbury.

CHAPTER XVII.

The Sunset Vision.

The General Conference of 1812—the first delegated convention of the Church—was looked forward to with concern by Asbury and the other Methodist leaders. It was expected that its actions would severely test the strength and utility of the constitution; but the session passed without stress or crucial issue. The new order followed the old, as one stage of life succeeds another. Methodism, which originated in a series of unmistakable providences, was not left to chance, nor to the unaided counsels of men in settling the enduring principles of its polity. The constitution, which developed out of experience and necessity, answered naturally to Methodist history and expansion.

This General Conference—the last which Asbury attended—was opened by him in the usual simple way —that is, with Scripture-reading, song, and prayer. Ninety delegates were seated in the audience room of the historic John Street Church, New York City. Rules of order, described as being a reduction of the Jeffersonian manual, were brought in, but were soon found to be cumbersome and impracticable, and so were promptly abandoned for a simpler and more common-sense code.

Bishop McKendree introduced very early in the session a departure which became a precedent in all subsequent General Conferences, and which has greatly helped to illuminate the paths of Methodist legislation. He submitted to the Conference a written address, setting forth his views on the state and needs of the connection. To this act of his colleague Asbury offered the objection that it was an innovation and needless; but after McKendree had briefly expounded his reasons for the step, the venerable man acquiesced with a smile. Later, on his own behalf, he addressed the Conference, through his colleague, in much the same spirit and also to much the same end. It was characteristic of Asbury that, self-sufficient though he was in his mastery of men and affairs, when shown the advantage of a new method or departure, he was quick to fall in with it, and nursed no sentiment of pride which prevented him from profiting by it to the fullest. An example of this was the spirit in which he finally abandoned the plan of a council for that of a delegated General Conference.

For a body so historically important the session of the General Conference of 1812 accomplished but little that was of lasting significance. There was, in fact, but little demand for new legislation. The validation of the joint action of the Bishops in creating the Genesee Conference, the division of the Western Conference into the Ohio and the Tennessee Conferences, the making of local deacons eligible to elders' orders, and a fresh refusal to take the appointment of the presiding elders out of the hands of the bishops and leave their selection to a majority vote of the Annual Conference practically outlines the work of the entire sitting.

Bishop Asbury had for some time had in contemplation a visit to his early home and friends in England, and had planned to begin his journey thither soon after the adjournment of the General Conference.

This had led Bishop McKendree to suggest in his address to the Conference the propriety of strengthening the episcopacy by the election of an additional bishop. Both the address of Bishop McKendree and the verbal communication of Bishop Asbury were referred to a committee styled "the Committee on Episcopacy," consisting of one member from each Annual Conference, an order which has ever since obtained. This committee reported unfavorably on the request of Bishop Asbury to be permitted to visit Europe, although it appeared that an invitation to do so had been extended him by the British Wesleyan Conference. Several reasons seem to have influenced the committee in denying this request. First, the confidence of the American preachers in Asbury's leadership was only equaled by their love for him. They also feared a repetition of the embarrassments which had come upon the connection through the continued absences of Bishop Coke. Should Asbury be given a leave of absence from the continent, it would mean, as they viewed it, a suspension for the time of his episcopal functions. That had been the rule applied to Coke, and they could not contemplate their patriarch in a similar situation with other feelings than those of personal distress. Just then, too, the shadows of the second war with Great Britain were deepening on the land, and hostilities actually began within the next few weeks. The whole truth is, the American preachers, one and all, felt that the cause they represented was safer when Asbury was near at hand and in their councils. He could not be spared.

The decision not to consent to Asbury's proposed European visit put an end to the scheme for electing

15

a third bishop. Asbury renewed his pledge to serve
the connection with all his powers of body and mind
as long and as largely as he could, and the incident
was closed.

The order of journey made by the two Bishops immediately following the General Conference was much
the same as in former years. It was up through
the Middle States, across New England, southward
through Western New York and Pennsylvania, into
the great valleys of the West, and back to the Atlantic
seaboard, in the Carolinas. The initial sessions of the
new Conferences—Ohio and Tennessee—were noteworthy incidents of the year. The former met in
Chillicothe, which brought Asbury back to a circle of
old friends and to the springs of tender memories.
On the journey southward he preached in the new
Statehouse at Frankfort and visited Louisville. Coming to Nashville, he found a neat new brick meetinghouse "thirty-four feet square, with galleries." This
was one of the half dozen predecessors of the present
McKendree Church, the "Jerusalem" house of Southern Methodism. From Nashville together the two
Bishops journeyed to Fountain Head, in Sumner
County, Tenn., where, in connection with a camp meeting, the Tennessee Conference was to be held. It was
on or near these grounds that, twenty-three years later,
the dust of McKendree was to find sepulture; and
though, after forty years, that dust was to be given a
new resting place on the campus of Vanderbilt University, the original marble slab still marks, as a ceno-
taph, the place where he slept.

The Conference which met at Charleston, S. C., in
December of this year, and which Asbury attended

with something of his old-time relish and exhilaration, is to be remembered as the session at which James O. Andrew was received on trial. The future bishop and destined divider of the world, a rustic lad of nineteen, almost wholly unlettered and wholly inexperienced, was not at the Conference, but awaited in his father's cabin in the eastern reaches of Georgia the scarcely hoped for tidings that he had been accepted as an itinerant Methodist preacher. The potencies which afterwards burst like a storm about the head of this man, and dissevered the house of Methodism, were then lying dormant in an ill-shaped and an ill-administered rule on African slavery. The age which might have anticipated and prevented the distresses of a future day lacked both the foresight and the unity demanded by its opportunity. But the room of history is large.

In June, 1813, seeing how his strength ebbed, Asbury made his will, naming as his executors Bishop McKendree, Daniel Hitt, Book Agent of the Church, and Henry Boehm, his faithful traveling companion. His estate, as he himself estimated it, was worth about two thousand dollars. This had come to him chiefly through the generosity of friends in Maryland. The whole sum was bequeathed to the Book Concern. "Let it return," he wrote, "and continue to aid the cause of piety." It is doing its work to-day in the apportioned publishing funds of the two Episcopal Methodisms.

In the course of this year's Conference visitations Asbury began to see the advantages of McKendree's plan for a cabinet of presiding elders in making the appointments. "The presiding eldership and the episcopacy saw eye to eye in the business of the stations," he wrote about this time; "there were no murmurings from the eighty-four employed."

This was the Bishop's last full year of work. He completed with McKendree the round of the inhabited republic, except the territory of Mississippi, and he still hoped to see this; but the time was come to relax. He had ridden five thousand miles during eight months, and had done the work of a bishop; but "on the peaceful banks of the Saluda" it came to him to write a valedictory address to the presiding elders, and to signify to his colleague that henceforth the burden was to weigh more heavily on his shoulders. This not that he meant to cease altogether from labors, but that he felt himself no longer able to bear the heavy crown of responsibility. He was ripe for release, but, like the aged St. John, he craved the joy of prophesying to the end. It was during this year that he met for the last time his faithful friend, Otterbein. The two venerable men had a long and soulful interview and an affectionate leave-taking. Shortly after this the great German leader was gathered to his fathers, remembered as a great and faithful leader.

In 1814 Henry Boehm found it necessary to terminate the arrangement he had made with Bishop Asbury to be his traveling companion. For five years he had been almost constantly at the side of the Methodist patriarch, and had come to know and share as few men had his thought and confidence. Many years afterwards, as has already been stated, he published the notes which he kept during his long attendance upon the heads of the Church, for Bishop McKendree was seldom himself separated from his colleague in his travels. The Boehm reminiscences have been most helpful in filling up the gaps in the history of the joint Asbury and McKendree administration.

Having lost the services of Boehm, Bishop Asbury applied to the Baltimore Conference for the detachment of one of its members to serve him in that stead. The choice fell upon John Wesley Bond. The selection was happy and fitting, and brought to the invalid during the remaining days of his life a congenial companionship and a faithful and tender ministry. Both Calvary and the Transfiguration were on the sufferer in those days. "I groan one minute in pain, and shout 'Glory!' the next." So he wrote, and so it was with him.

And now came to Asbury a sorrow such as he had not felt since the death of Wesley. While on a mission voyage to India, Thomas Coke died and was buried in the Indian Ocean, eastward off the Cape of Good Hope. Bishop Coke is not only entitled to be called the foreign minister of Methodism, but his claim to a place amongst the very first and greatest missionaries of the world is beyond dispute. In 1813 he completed a plan for planting missionary stations across half the world. To this enterprise he pledged his private fortune, which was not small. Also he succeeded in committing to his enterprise a goodly number of his Wesleyan brethren. With these, having obtained the indorsement of the British Conference, he set sail in December for Ceylon; but on May 2, 1814, he expired, and his body was given the sea for a mausoleum. His companions went on with the enterprise, and established in India the mission stations that in their growth have made the Wesleyan Church one of the greatest missionary forces of the world. The news of the death of his former colleague did not reach Asbury until many months after it occurred. The testimony which he bore to his memory was characteristic and eloquent. In his journal stand these words: "Thomas Coke, of the third branch of Oxonian Methodists; as a minister of Christ, in zeal, in labors, and in services, the greatest man of the last century."

A new feature of comfort was added to Asbury's western journey in the year 1814. Sometime early in the year friends in Philadelphia presented him with "a light four-wheeled carriage." This was the "chaise" in which he made his last episcopal visitation, and in which he rode until "the horsemen of Israel" hailed him for the ascent of the skies.

At the Ohio Conference he attempted to preside, Bishop McKendree having been so seriously crippled by a fall from his horse as not to be able to be present. The task, however, proved too much for his strength, so he resigned both the chair and the stations into the hands of John Sale, an elder, who had been elected by the Conference to preside. The presbyter easily met the demands of the post. The success of this necessary expedient gave Asbury great satisfaction. "The Conferences are now out of their infancy," he mused; "their rulers can now be called from amongst themselves." As a father who, unmindful of the growth of his sons that move about him from day to day, awakes from a life dream to see his offspring standing shoulder to shoulder with himself, so Asbury awoke to find his spiritual sons of a stature that he had not noted. Except in worth and wisdom of soul, there were many about him who easily overtopped his own venerable head.

At the Tennessee Conference, a month later, he stood more firmly on his feet, and would have set out from that point for the far-away Natchez stations, but Bishop McKendree's disabled condition rendered such a course impossible. Within a fortnight Asbury's strength had again failed, and he was admonished that the end of his pilgrimage was near. From October, 1814, to October, 1815, he dragged a constantly halting and suffering body around his wonted circuit of six to eight thousand miles; but it was no more to utter the voice of command, but to say farewells to those who should see his face no more. Everywhere he spoke words of tenderness and warning, and preached the message of perfect love. "The time is short," was a refrain in his sermons which all men remembered. One who saw him about this time wrote of him thus: "In appearance he was a picture of plainness and simplicity: an old man spare and tall, but remarkably clean, with a plain frock coat, drab or mixed waistcoat, and small clothes of the same kind, a neat stock, a broad-brimmed hat, with an uncommon low crown; while his white locks, venerable with age, added a simplicity to his appearance it is not easy to describe."

True to his practical instincts, even in these tottering days, he carried around the continent his favorite "mite" subscription list for the relief of the ministry— a feeble but well-meant means for supplying the gigantic defects of a primitive and mistakenly conceived system of Church finance.

Nearing the seaboard in 1815, he learned with joy of the treaty of peace which ended the second war with Great Britain. A few days later his patriotic resentment was stirred by a sight of the charred ruins of the President's house and the Capitol at Washington. Twice had his heart—once in his prime and then in his old age—supported contending emotions of love and loyalty for his native land and the land of his adoption; and this also had brought him a measure of perfection.

Passing through Virginia, he had been entertained by the fourth generation of the Jarratts, whose fellowship awakened within him memories of the early revival which in a time of trial had strengthened his soul and fixed his purpose to remain in America. Now he saw again "Perry Hall," and for the last time rested his weary body within its hallowed walls. Some weeks later he was at Croton, in the State of New York, the home of his great and influential friend, Governor Van Cortlandt; but the mighty man of faith and deeds had gone to his rest. A voice was speaking above the sleeping dust, but a living voice called the weary apostle onward. The cessation of war had again opened the gate to Canada, and he had already laid special plans for the rehabilitation of the work beyond the St. Lawrence. At the New England Conference, which he had undertaken to hold in the absence of Bishop McKendree, he was unable to preside, and George Pickering filled the chair, and sat with the cabinet in stationing the preachers.

By a shortened line of travel the Bishop and his companion returned to Maryland, where he completed the revision of his journal. Of this journal he says: "As a record of the early history of Methodism in America, it will be of use, and, accompanied by the Minutes of the Conference, will tell all that will be necessary to know. I have buried in shades all that will be proper to forget."

The summertide was now at its height, and the genial sunshine had stayed a little the course of his malady. He rallied perceptibly, and entered upon his last journey to the West in comparative comfort of body; but the winds of autumn that met him in the distant Ohio Valley quickly relegated him to his former condition of all but helpless invalidism. Blistering and bleeding were his remedies for anæmia and inanition. Unbelievable empiricism! Incredible credulity of the age! But suffering many things both of his disorders and his physicians, the uncomplaining invalid crept on, distributing Testaments when he could not preach and disbursing amongst his needy brethren the mite fund which he had collected with infinite patience and zeal.

While journeying from Ohio toward the seat of the Tennessee Conference through the succession of rich valleys that made the virgin land, he heard voices calling through the soft autumn winds, and saw doors opening through the glory of blue horizons and through uplooming hills, dappled with the hues of changing foliage. "This western part of the empire," he said to McKendree, "will be the glory of America. There should be five Conferences marked out here." One of his later successors in office, commenting on these words, says: "Where he would have been content with five Conferences, we now have fifty." So have the people called Methodists multiplied and replenished the lands. But the voices which Asbury heard and the visions which he saw did not deceive him; he saw the future unfold its wonders, but he saw not all.

The Tennessee Conference session fell at Bethlehem, near Lebanon, in the early days of October, 1815. It was Asbury's last Conference. He arrived in his chaise in good time, but was unable either to preside or to arrange the stations. He preached on the Sabbath and ordained the deacons. With that he laid down the episcopal office. His journal carries the sad record in these words: "My eyes fail; I resign the stations to Bishop McKendree; I will take away my feet."

One earthly wish remained. It was to meet the General Conference called to sit in Baltimore the following May. For the long journey thither he husbanded his strength. Nearly two scores of times he had scaled the Appalachian barriers. For thirty-one successive years, with a single break, he had visited the valleys of the Holston and the Cumberland. They were to him what Hebron was to Caleb—a southland with springs of water. But now from the heights of "the Alps" he took his last view of them. A sigh of regret and a shout of triumph mingled his emotions, and he set his face toward Maryland, after having foregone his dream of a midwinter rest in Charleston.

During his slow progress through South Carolina he completed as far as he was able an address for the General Conference and a communication to Bishop McKendree. He also dictated a lengthy letter to Rev. Joseph Benson, of the English Conference, the original of which is now in my possession in the hand of an amanuensis. As it was unsigned, it is almost certain that it was never transmitted to the great commentator.

The last entry made in his journal was on December 7, 1815; but it was the twentieth day of the month before he finally abandoned the hope of reaching Charleston and turned northward. He was then near the middle of the State of South Carolina; but though he traveled as the weather and his strength permitted, so feeble was he and so frequently was his companion constrained to halt that he might rest, they reached Richmond, Va., only at the end of three months. Frequently during this stage of his journey he attempted to preach, but his voice was too weak to be heard except by those near his person. However, having arrived at Richmond with his traveling companion, on Monday, March 18, he announced his purpose to speak to the congregation in the old meetinghouse on the following Sabbath. Friends undertook to dissuade him from this course, but his reply was that he had a special call to give his testimony in that place. Strong and loyal hands lifted him into his carriage and he was driven to the door of the sanctuary he loved. Again he was tenderly lifted and borne into the church, where a chair had been placed for him upon a table within the chancel. Thus seated he discoursed for nearly an hour, and with surprisingly sustained voice and power, from Romans ix. 28: "For he will finish the work, and cut it short in righteousness: because a short work will the Lord make upon the earth." It was his last sermon —in fact, his last public ministration of any kind. When the feebly kindled glow of action left his frame, the chill of death set in. But the hope—the purpose—to reach, ere death should seal his eyes, the green shores of the Chesapeake still reigned in the soul of the saint and patriot. During the next five days, riding in their closed carriage, he and his companion covered fifty-seven additional miles of their way. The final halt was made at the home of George Arnold, an old and often visited friend. The place was twenty miles short of the city of Fredericksburg, which the travelers had hoped to reach by the succeeding Sabbath. On Saturday the Bishop showed extreme feebleness, and passed a restless night, but refused to permit the calling of a physician. Early the next day he frankly expressed his belief that the end was at hand. Being asked by his companion if he had any word to leave for the Conference or his colleague, his reply was that he had already written and spoken so fully that further word was unnecessary.

Asking the hour of the day, and being told that it was the hour of eleven, he requested that the family and his companion gather in his chamber for worship. Strangely and significantly enough, the Scripture lesson for the evening of that day in the Sunday service was the last chapter of the Revelation. This chapter Bond read and expounded, the closing lesson of the day closing the days of the labors of that faithful, simple life. "During the whole of the meeting," wrote Bond, "his soul seemed much engaged. He appeared much elevated, and raised his hands frequently in token of triumph." Truly affecting was his direction given to Bond to "read the mite subscription," thus showing that he remembered the toiling missionaries even in his dying moments. Being told that only the family was present, he said no more. His voice had failed. Asked if he still found the Master precious, he lifted his hands toward heaven, and "then, without a groan or a complaint," yielded up his spirit to God. The solemn scene was closed on the moment of four o'clock in the afternoon of the Sabbath, March 31, 1816, as is learned from the letter of Bond to Bishop McKendree.

He was buried, with simple undertaking and ceremony, in the family burying ground of his host and friend, George Arnold, and only a few rods from the door of the cottage in which he expired. A month later, when the General Conference met in Baltimore, plans were completed to have his body exhumed* and buried in a grave under the pulpit of Eutaw Street Church, in Baltimore. On the 9th of May the body arrived under escort of Philip Bruce, Nelson Reed, Freeborn Garrettson, Lewis Myers, and George Pickering. A guard of honor was detailed from the Conference to watch the casket that night, during which time it rested in Light Street Church. The next day

---

*In June of the year 1907, under the direction of Rev. Charles D. Bulla, pastor of the Church at Alexandria, Va., the Epworth Leaguers of the Washington District, Methodist Episcopal Church, South, erected upon the site of the George Arnold house a marble marker to which it is hoped in the not distant future to add an equestrian statue of the "Pioneer Bishop." Dr. Bulla gives the following account of the pilgrimage and transaction: "It was at Fredericksburg that our Leaguers of the Washington District met June 25, 1907. All that was needed to make a good Conference was there—a goodly number, a cordial welcome, hospitality at its best, a carefully arranged program, every speaker present and prepared. There was also spirit in everything, not a dull moment from beginning to end, and enough in reserve for double the time. It was an Asburian Conference and Pilgrimage. Early Thursday morning, June 27, conveyances carried our League pilgrims to Spottsylvania Courthouse, twelve miles southwest of Fredericksburg. We journeyed on four miles to the southwest of Spottsylvania Courthouse to the site of the George Arnold house. The Leaguers of the Washington District had

a solemn procession of twenty thousand people, led by Bishop McKendree and William Black, the representative of British Methodism to the General Conference, followed the holy dust to its new resting place. Of kindred in blood, there was none to mourn; but Henry Boehm and John Wesley Bond, his "sons" in long and dutiful ministries, stood by the coffin as chief mourners, while thousands of hearts besides in silence reverenced with mingled sorrow and gladness the memory of the illustrious dead. Bishop McKendree delivered a brief discourse, "full of pathos and embracing some of the leading facts of his history and traits of character," after which the casket was lowered into the vault. In June, 1854, the remains of Asbury were again disinterred and buried in Mount Olivet Ceme-

---

secured the plot of ground on which the house stood and erected upon it a granite marker five feet in height bearing this inscription:

ON THIS SPOT
STOOD THE HOME OF GEORGE ARNOLD,
WHERE
BISHOP FRANCIS ASBURY
DIED MARCH 31, 1816.
ERECTED BY THE EPWORTH LEAGUES
OF THE WASHINGTON DISTRICT,
BALTIMORE CONFERENCE, METHODIST EPISCOPAL CHURCH,
SOUTH, DECEMBER, 1906.

In the shade of a large walnut tree we held our service. We sang John Wesley's noble lyric, 'How happy is the pilgrim's lot;' read the twenty-first chapter of Revelation, the scripture expounded by John Wesley Bond, at Bishop Asbury's request, the day he died; an address on the 'Life and Character of Francis Asbury,' another on the 'Gospel Ministry;' concluding with a consecration service in which a large number participated."

tery, Baltimore, where are the graves of Robert Straw-bridge and Jesse Lee, as also those of not a few others of Methodism's unforgotten dead.

Speech cannot perfectly portray the lineaments of the righteous, nor make wholly real to thought the miracles of their deeds and sacrifices. The martyrs and confessors are but little perceived aside from the nimbuses and aureoles that encompass them. The spiritual, the world-changing forces that informed the souls of the mighty dead are elusive to our busy and too often enslaved thoughts. St. Paul is better known to the average Christian by his long travels, the scourgings which he received, and the imprisonments which he suffered than by his doctrines or the silent mastery of his deathless soul. Perhaps it comes of human limitations—our necessary dependence upon the tangible as a means of reaching the unseen, the spiritual. Francis Asbury has been dead less than a century; but it is only the picture of the pioneer Bishop tirelessly tracing the continent on horseback, in sulky, or in chaise that popularly survives. The apostolic spirit that, moving from land to land, drew about it the destinies of a mighty people, and shaped, to an extent which the hands of none other were permitted to shape, a civilization Christian at heart because that heart was preached into it—that spirit is but faintly seen by modern American eyes. Two hundred and seventy thousand miles he traveled during his episcopate, preached sixteen thousand sermons, ordained four thousand ministers, and sat as the president of two hundred and twenty-four Annual Conferences. Prodigious accomplishment! And yet it is beyond even this circumstance of figures that we must seek the true Asbury.

The circuit of his power and influence is to the ends of our history; and though it cannot be so confidently said of him as Southey said of Wesley, that millenniums hence the influence of his life and work will be felt and acknowledged, the days that shall witness to him are yet many in the centuries to be.

INDEX.